FESTIVE MARYLAND RECIPES

HOLIDAY TRADITIONS *from the* OLD LINE STATE

KARA MAE HARRIS

Copyright © 2023 by Kara Mae Harris
Recipes 2023 by Rachel Rappaport
Recipe accompanying text © 2023 by Rachel Rappaport

Book Design by Sara Tomko
Illustrations by Ben Claassen, III

All rights reserved

For information about permission to reproduce selections from this book, contact Kara Mae Harris, kara@karamae.com.

ISBN 979-8-218-09854-4
LCCN: 2023902814

Published by Old Line Plate
Baltimore Maryland
Oldlineplate.com

SPECIAL THANKS TO:

Special thanks to the Jewish Museum of Maryland,
Sarah Hedlund at Montgomery History,
Special Collections and the Maryland Room at the Enoch Pratt Free Library,
Kana Jenkins at Hornbake Library of University of Maryland,
Joe Tropea at Maryland Center for History and Culture,
Yechiel Wolgel, Webster Phillips, Dr. Katie Labor, and Sheila Wells for proofreading.

Colossal gratitude to Rachel, Sara, Ben, and Chef Shields
for believing in this project from the start.

FOREWORD
John Shields

Chef John Shields—known as the Culinary Ambassador of the Chesapeake Bay—began his cooking career at an early age alongside his grandmother Gertie Cleary and has never looked back. John has owned several restaurants and currently co-owns Gertrude's Chesapeake Kitchen at the Baltimore Museum of Art. The host of two PBS cooking shows, and author of several books including *The Chesapeake Bay Cookbook, Coastal Cooking with John Shields,* and *The New Chesapeake Kitchen,* Shields recently founded a non-profit, Our Common Table. Its mission is about rebuilding our local food economy through education and promotion of a bay and body friendly lifestyle that brings us all to a "common table."

One of our classic, iconic Maryland cookbooks' title says it best when summing up our regional food - Eat, Drink, and Be Merry In Maryland. Kara Mae Harris brings this call-to-action to life in her new work chronicling the vast treasure of recipes and storytelling she has collected over the years.

You don't need to convince me about the amazing food we Marylanders prepare to celebrate all the festive occasions of life. We celebrate everything that life brings - holidays, ceremonies, holy days, sporting games - all the while marking time and each season with food. And what better place to be located than Maryland, which produces, and is home to, the bounty of the Chesapeake Bay region.

I grew up in Baltimore many years ago and have fond memories of the food and the celebrations connected. I also was fortunate to grow up in a city that was on the cusp of both the urban and agricultural. The legendary municipal public markets - Lexington, Cross Street, North Avenue, Belair, Broadway, Hollins, Northeast, and Richmond, to name a few, were overflowing with the culinary treasures of the region. They were the original "farmers markets." The bustling port city was ringed with farmland and even suburban truck farms as close as Baltimore and Anne Arundel counties. The array of produce, meat, poultry, dairy, and seafood was astounding.

These are the ingredients that brought Maryland food to the forefront of the culinary world. The recipes were shaped by waves of immigrants, enslaved people, and the native tribes that made the tributaries of the Chesapeake and Maryland their home. It is a rich culinary tapestry that is the foundation of a true, regional-American cuisine.

The people of Maryland introduce many of the recipes in this book through their words and images. The finest examples of Maryland cuisine are found in the kitchens of watermen, farmers, proprietors of small back-road inns and taverns, and most especially at community events where locals come together to celebrate the seasonal holidays, rites of passage, and their common love for the Chesapeake Bay. We can't talk about Maryland food without talking about the Bay.

Years ago I wrote my first cookbook on the region, The Chesapeake Bay Cookbook and in doing my research I traveled the 200 plus miles of the Bay. I visited with folks that had roots here for well over 200 years and others who had more recently arrived. All were proud of the culinary traditions from the countries that they had come from. And, they all had stories. You cannot truly understand Maryland cuisine without these stories.

And this is where Kara Mae Harris comes in. For the past seven years Kara has single handedly chronicled

Lexington Market

thousands of historically significant Maryland recipes with staunch determination, passion, and a sense of joy. Many of you I am sure are fans of her phenomenal blog - Old Line Plate. And if you are not yet acquainted by all means check it out - it is a culinary treasure.

Kara has not only chronicled countless Maryland recipes but has spent thousands of hours researching our collective culinary heritage. Her voluminous first book, Old Line Plate, is a treasure trove of historic Maryland cooking and contains authentic recipes from the 17th, 18th, 19th, and 20th centuries. The early recipes collected during the time that these United States were being formed give insight to the times and the recipes are terrific fun to read, although some are difficult to transfer to a 21st century kitchen.

Here in Festive Maryland Recipes Kara is working to make these time honored recipes work in our home kitchen. She has enlisted the help of the talented Rachel Rapaport, animator of the delightful Coconut & Lime blog. Each of the recipes included are works unto themselves. Kara's descriptive recipe background and engaging storytelling brings the recipes and their histories to life. The actual "old-recipe" transfiguration, and updated methodology is splendid.

It will make the reader, like myself, chomping at the bit to get into the kitchen to start cooking. The wheel of time continues for Maryland celebrations and festivities. And this book will help bring back memories to some, and make new memories for many more.

INTRODUCTION
Kara Mae Harris

Holidays are times of joy and respite but also reflection and gratitude.

"PREPARE FOR THE HOLIDAYS," read a small headline in the *Democratic Advocate of Westminster*, Maryland on December 7th, 1872. The anonymous author broadcasted their excitement: "Thanksgiving past, Christmas is next in order."

"The sauerkraut and the 'apple butter' (what a pity we can't find a better name for this popular edible) are already laid up in store;" they continued, "fat turkeys and cranberry sauce, with crisp and well-bleached celery are now to be looked after; and links of luscious sausage… and the dish of hot smoking hominy, white as the driven snow - that good old Maryland morsel… the cookies, and the fosnots, and the buns and the caramels, the plum puddings and the mince pies…"

The article went on to mention "trinkets and trifles," Christmas trees, and stockings, but the point had been made. Holidays equal food, and this writer was hankering for it.

The press in Maryland was always standing at the ready to rhapsodize about something good to eat— better still if the food had the patriotic luster of 'Marylandness' about it.

These reminiscences of food give us insight into the culture of our state, but they rarely paint the whole picture. The magic, for them, was in the eating.

Buried within the women's pages of these same newspapers you can sometimes find recipes. They are straightforward and sparse. For the people who clipped and cooked these recipes, a few ingredients and brief instructions were enough to spark the imagination, placing the home cooks within their role in the memories soon to be made.

Cooking takes on an air of ritual for holidays. People will reserve beloved treats, depriving themselves of a specific flavor until one special day, bestowing the food with honor and respect. Others may recreate dishes they don't even like, year after year, in the name of tradition. The cooking process is a ceremony with the power to confer a blessing from the dead to the living.

This doesn't mean that new traditions can't be made, nor old ones left behind. That power is in our hands. To paraphrase historian Michael Twitty, food doesn't give us meaning— we give meaning to our food.

Despite my enthusiastic support for any impulse to enact new institutions, or to resurrect old ones, I'm always surprised to hear when people cook recipes from my Old Line Plate blog. I often advise against it.

This has made me reflect. Do I not trust readers to follow these vague old recipes?

Ultimately, I realized that it's the thought of any resulting disappointment that bothers me. I don't want a bad meal served on my account.

And so, I decided I should finally enlist a professional to make some historical recipes worthy of perpetuation.

When I want to find a recipe for coddies or smearcase —a recipe that readers can reliably follow— I always turn to Rachel Rapaport's Coconut & Lime blog. Aside from being the author of one of the longest-running original recipe blogs, Rachel is a Marylander and a Baltimorean through and through. She knows what these dishes should taste like and how to help her readers recreate them without complication or pretense. I was honored when she accepted my invitation to be a part of this book. Her influence on it goes above and beyond the recipe text.

The original recipes in this collection come from Maryland cookbooks in my own collection and in libraries. This presents a huge limitation as to the scope of "holiday" diversity that can be reflected. By far, the majority of community cookbooks were created by Judeo-Christian churches with middle-class white congregations. My project is a tiny sample; a magnifying glass over an area of culinary history that is accessible to me.

Many Maryland families at the turn of the 20th century would not consider a proper Christmas dinner without oyster stew.

Similarly, Old Line Plate readers can expect a recipe to come with a preachy warning about the dangers of nostalgia. Our past may have been delicious, but it wasn't pretty.

Maryland was once world-famous for a dining culture of oysters, waterfowl, crab and terrapin, served in preparations that had been crafted by the hands of the enslaved. In postbellum times, the cuisine of Maryland gained prestige. The mystique was based not only around the dishes themselves but in casting the talent behind them in a paradoxical pigeonhole of subservience: supernaturally gifted rather than highly trained and skilled; put on a pedestal yet belittled; a dual status befitting the "middling temperament" of a state that remained in the Union while upholding the status quo on slavery.

This reality confronts me in my research again and again. Fond memories of "colonial kitchens," "faithful servants," and "attentive Mammies" were often expressed right alongside the plum puddings, old hams and turkeys; the Christmas holly and evergreen boughs.

In compiling these recipes I hope to bolster an appreciation of the unique and treasured foods of Maryland, but I do not want to perpetuate the gleeful ignorance that many Marylanders once served up with our food. Holidays are times of joy and respite but also reflection and gratitude.

As seen in these pages, the fall and winter months bear the majority of holidays. The reason for this lies in our agrarian past. From fall harvest to lean winter months when sharing was a necessity, we gathered to commemorate the miracle of our mere survival. Winter also stirs a need to light up dark days and spend time with loved ones.

I hope these recipes encourage just that, filling kitchens with warmth and aroma, and instilling cooks with satisfaction, generosity, and the mysterious forces of holiday magic.

HOW TO USE THIS BOOK

Each dish is comprised of two parts:

One part essay written by **Kara Mae Harris** and one part modernized recipe developed by **Rachel Rappaport**.

The whole aims to provide readers with the historical background and cultural context of the dish while supplying an accompanying recipe you can create on your own using ingredients found in today's grocery stores and kitchens.

And remember: some of these recipes may have originated around the world, but they found new forms in Maryland. Authenticity is subjective.

FESTIVE MARYLAND: CONTENTS

Kasha mit Varnishkes	11
Chicken & Pastry	14
Stuffed Ham	18
Sauerkraut for Thanksgiving	24
Turkey Stuffed with Oysters	28
Apple Toddy	32
White Potato Pies	34
Plum Pudding	38
Oyster Stew	43
Wassail Bowl	46
Cornish Saffron Bread	47
Barley Casserole (Kuba)	50
Hoppin John	53
Egg Nog	58
New Year's Cakes	62
Chop-Chae	67
Kinklings	73
Ginger Cream Cake	78
Chocolate Macaroons	84
Easter Pies	88
Koulourakia (Easter Cookies)	92
Blintzes	96
Strawberry Cobbler	99
Biblography	104

Temple Shalom
KASHA MIT VARNISHKES

When Joseph Steinberg's family moved to Rockville in 1908, there were no other Jewish families in town. In 1984, he described how he had to take chickens to a kosher butcher for slaughter. "In the Jewish faith… we don't chop the heads off," he explained. "We have to do a little fancy number at the throat, but… you have to be a rabbi, sort of, to do that. The nearest man that had the license was up in Gaithersburg."

Kosher Butcher Shop

Steinberg commuted by streetcar to Hebrew school in Washington D.C., and his family traveled up to Baltimore to observe holidays with a larger Jewish community.

In an exchange that would be repeated by subsequent generations in Montgomery County, Steinberg assisted his friends with Christmas tree trimming and he enjoyed Christmas candy, and in turn, his Christian friends learned about Hanukkah candle lighting and spinning the Dreidel.

Morty Sclar, a resident of Silver Spring in the 1930s, similarly described his family traveling to Washington D.C. for kosher foods, and making wine in their basement for Passover.

In these and other oral histories given to the city of Rockville, elder Jewish citizens told of the great lengths families went to in order to keep kosher, and of the holidays spent with their relatives in Baltimore.

Gradually, the Jewish population of the area grew alongside that of the D.C. suburbs. The Montgomery County that Steinberg left behind with his 2001 passing was a place of many customs and backgrounds, with Jewish citizens comprising up to 10% of county residents.

Temple Shalom, established in Chevy Chase in the 1950s, was the second Reform congregation in the county. Today, its website is a reflection of the greater D.C. area, with an emphasis on diversity and welcome.

The 1970s cookbook from the Sisterhood of Temple Shalom includes a section in the back entitled "What Mama Used To Make." Suggested dishes for particular holidays are laid out in a chart, many showing alternate spellings- Blintzes and Cheese Cake for Shavuos; Hamantashen pastries for Purim; for Passover, Gefilte Fish, Chicken Soup with Knadlach, and Sponge Cake; for Rosh Hashanah, Honey Cake and Carrot Tsimmes. Also included is a recipe for Kasha Mit Varnishkes - a dish popularly served at Rosh Hashanah and other holidays.

The recipe's author Phyllis Nehmer (1923-2014) moved to Silver Spring from Pennsylvania in 1946. By then, the area had a sizable Jewish community of which Nehmer was an active member. The Temple has a fund honoring the memory of Phyllis and her husband Stanley, dedicated to "special events and programming to expand Judaic knowledge, social interaction, continuing education, and arts enrichment."

Possibly originating in Eastern Europe, kasha varnishkes can be found on deli menus throughout the capital region today. Author and historian Michel Twitty, who was raised in Montgomery County, wrote in his 2022 book "Koshersoul: The Faith and Food Journey of an African American Jew," "when people ask me about my favorite 'Jewish' food, I say kasha varnishkes... It's the best of the earth in one bowl."

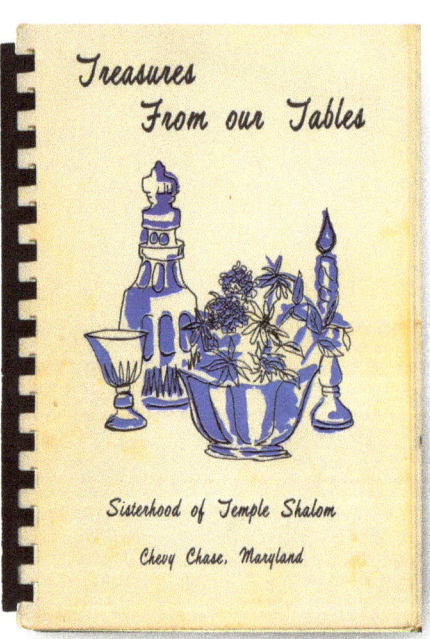

In 2021, the Washington Post printed a recipe, calling kasha varnishkes "flexible enough to work with vegetarian, vegan or gluten-free eating preferences." Like people, food migrates and changes while remaining grounded in history. —KMH

Kasha Varnishkes

Yields 6–8 servings

SCHMALTZ

side dish

Montgomery County

This is a very simple but filling side dish. Traditionally, and most deliciously, you would use rendered chicken fat (schmaltz) to sauté the onions. If you don't have it handy, substitute your favorite cooking oil. Don't be scared to really cook those onions, this is where the flavor comes from, you want it slightly smoky, not sweet. —RR

INGREDIENTS:

- 2 tablespoons schmaltz
- 1 large onion, chopped
- 1 cup kasha (buckwheat groats)
- 1 egg
- 2 cups chicken stock
- ¾ lb bow tie noodles, cooked and drained

DIRECTIONS:

In a large saucepan, sauté **onions** in **schmaltz** over medium-high heat until nearly blackened, about 20 minutes.

Meanwhile, mix the **egg** and **kasha** in a small bowl. Add the mixture to the onions and sauté with onions until the kernels begin to separate, about 5-10 minutes.

Add **broth** and then cover.

Simmer over low heat until kasha is tender.

Salt and pepper to taste.

Remove from heat.

Stir in noodles and serve.

Elizabeth Locklear (Lumbee)

Lumbee

CHICKEN & PASTRY

In 1981, the Baltimore Sun interviewed Elizabeth Locklear about cooking and food. Locklear was one of approximately 4,000 Lumbee tribe members living in the Baltimore area at the time. Like many of them, Locklear made frequent trips to the tribal homeland in Robeson County, North Carolina, where she stocked up on corn meal, liver pudding, and fresh vegetables. She had also begun to make spaghetti and lasagna because her son was dating an Italian girl. "I don't use a cookbook," she told the Sun.

Alongside the interview, the paper printed her recipes for fry bread, Indian corn pudding, squash fritters, and Lumbee Sweet Potato Pie.

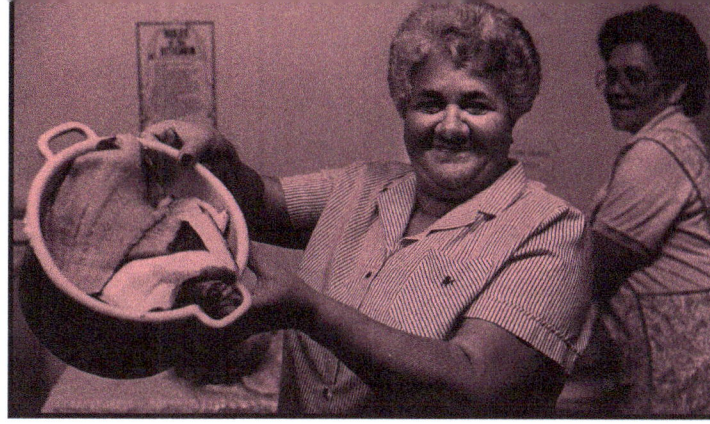

Dosha Jacobs (Lumbee) and Virgina "Love" Locklear (Lumbee)

Kirby Locklear (Lumbee)

Sweet potato pie is the most-circulated recipe associated with the Lumbee. The Old Line Plate database contains a recipe from the 1994 Baltimore Orioles cookbook "Gourmet Bird Feed," contributed by six-time All-Star Harold Baines. Baines biographies do not mention Lumbee heritage, but he wrote "I'm not much of a dessert eater, but I indulge myself in this recipe."

Lumbee Sweet Potato Pie can still be found in Baltimore at Rose's Bakery in Northeast Market. Rosie Bowen, who took over the bakery her father started, famously makes them using sweet potatoes from North Carolina. Like Locklear once did, Bowen visits family in Lumberton and comes back with items she can't find in Baltimore, including cornmeal. Locklear and Bowen both told interviewers that the texture of the cornmeal was different from what is available in Maryland.

Another specialty of Rose's Bakery is the Lumbee version of chicken and dumplings, known as Chicken and Pastry.

"It's a Sunday dinner thing," Bowen told me in a phone conversation, "but also for special occasions. Definitely holidays."

Bowen is a food history enthusiast, observing the unique and changing food traditions of Baltimore from the vantage point of her bakery.

Her home neighborhood has long been a dynamic confluence of immigrants. Neighborhoods like Corned Beef Row, Little Italy, and Little Bohemia once overlapped with what became known as "The Reservation," home to an influx of Lumbee families from North Carolina.

Bowen's cousin, historian and artist Ashley Minner, has been preserving the history of The Reservation with research, walking tours, and oral histories. Minner's work is not only focused on the past, but also the continued presence of the Lumbee in and around the strip of Baltimore Street that many sought out when they migrated to Maryland starting in the 1940s.

"When you look at food," Bowen said, "everyone has their own versions. You could put people from all over the world in a room with the same ingredients but each has their own way of making and seasoning it." She sees this now with the cuisine of the many Latin Americans who have more recently made East Baltimore their home.

Although Chicken and Pastry was frequently mentioned in The Robesonian newspaper of Lumberton, North Carolina in the 1960s, it did not publish any recipes until the early 2000s. This was a family favorite that presumably everyone knew how to make. Historians and folkway preservationists like Bowen and Minner are working to bring this cherished dish to the wider public in Maryland.

As I gathered recipes for this book, intending to represent as much of the state as could, I noticed a disproportionate number of them came from East Baltimore. I thought about the different families living from one block to the next, and ultimately accepted this seeming imbalance.

Wherever they came from and whyever they ended up in Maryland, people brought with them the desire to serve up a taste of their old home in their new one. —KMH

Chicken n' Pastry

fat and flavor

Baltimore City

Yields 6–8 servings

BUTTER

main dish

When you talk about Lumbee food, Chicken n' Pastry is always one of the first dishes that comes up. It's simple, it's delicious, and can be made with very basic ingredients while still feeling holiday-special.

The recipe shared with us had canned cream of chicken soup in it. Which is totally fine, of course, and a valid shortcut to a creamy dish. It was a cold, rainy December day when I wanted to work on this recipe and while I eat many cans of soup for lunch each year, I don't normally keep the "recipe" kind around. My guess is that originally it was made with just a fatty old hen (to give it the traditional yellow color) and some vegetables until someone realized they could use a shelf-stable product instead of having to chop anything up or rely on having fresh aromatics on hand.

Luckily, I did have chicken and flour and a couple of other basics and that's really all you need. I'm hoping this version will satisfy traditionalists, canned soup lovers, and canned soup skeptics alike. I've sped it up a little by using thighs instead of a whole chicken but don't be tempted to use boneless, skinless, or breasts. You need that fat and flavor. —RR

INGREDIENTS:

- 2½ lbs skin-on, bone-in chicken thighs
- 1 onion, chopped
- 2 stalks celery (with leaves), chopped
- 2 bay leaves
- 2 quarts water or chicken stock
- Salt
- Freshly ground black pepper
- 2 cups flour
- 1 teaspoon baking powder
- ¼ cup cold butter, cut into small chunks

DIRECTIONS:

Place the **chicken, onion, celery, bay leaf, seasoning, and the water** or stock in a large stock pot. Add more water or stock if needed to cover the chicken. Bring to a boil, reduce heat, cover, and cook until chicken is cooked through about 25 minutes.

Remove the chicken and bay leaf from the pot, leaving the broth to simmer. Remove 1 cup of broth to a shallow bowl. Set that aside to cool while you work on the chicken.

Discard the bay leaf. Skin, debone, and shred the chicken. Discard the skin and bones. Place the meat in a large, covered bowl to keep warm.

In a large mixing bowl, whisk together **flour** and **baking powder**. Using your hands, work in the butter until it resembles coarse, wet sand. Add the cooled stock and stir until it looks like dough. It will be stiff like pie dough so a hand mixer might help.

Lightly flour a clean, flat surface and roll out pastry to ⅛-inch. Cut pastry into ½-inch wide by 1 ½ inch long strips.

Bring the contents of the stock pot to a rolling boil. Slowly drop in the **pastry cut-outs**. Reduce the heat and simmer for about 15 minutes, stirring occasionally so the pastry doesn't turn into one big lump. **Stir in the reserved shredded chicken**. Simmer 10 more minutes or until the chicken is hot again and the pastry is cooked through.

Serve immediately.

HOLIDAY TRADITIONS FROM THE OLD LINE STATE

St. Mary's County
STUFFED HAM

FESTIVE MARYLAND RECIPES

It's hard to describe the flavor of Southern Maryland Stuffed Ham: salty ham brimming with cabbage and kale; mustard and celery seed; the lingering sting of hot red pepper. But it's so much more than that. To those who have tasted it, it seems like a mystery that stuffed ham hasn't caught on more beyond St. Mary's County. Until you try to make it.

There are many newspaper articles about stuffed ham, but the St. Mary's College Slackwater Center oral histories offer some of the most detailed personal accounts. Interviewees talk about growing greens to stuff the ham with, personal preferences, learning to make the ham, and of course their own processes. An interview with one Mary Drury of the Clements community goes into the most detail, describing "the tedious job, almost agony sometimes, of stuffing it until you have as much stuffing in there as you can get in the ham."

Theresa Young and Mary Woodyard in 2005

Jane Frances Swales

HOLIDAY TRADITIONS FROM THE OLD LINE STATE

I certainly don't find it "agonizing" but it IS a lot of work.

I've been fortunate enough to sample the ham made by Bertha Hunt, daughter of Theresa Young, who was one of the authors of "300 Years of Black Cooking in St. Mary's County."

Young contributed a dozen or so recipes (or rather, approximations of her proportions and techniques) to the 1975 cookbook, which was a fundraiser for Citizens for Progress, a local anti-poverty organization that she also co-founded.

That cookbook was just a small piece in a lifetime of service but it has become a cherished regional classic, drawing attention to the other aspects of her life and legacy.

In Bertha's living room hangs a series of family portraits. A color photograph of her mother is at the center. At the end of the row is a black-and-white picture of Alice Toney, Bertha's great-great-grandmother, who was born enslaved on the nearby Blackistone plantation. The portraits are visible from the kitchen counter where Bertha prepares her ham.

Early ties to plantations run by Catholic Jesuit priests mean that Stuffed Ham's whitewashed origin has been associated with Easter. The 1983 Southern Heritage "Family Gatherings" cookbook said "The good priests, having tired of a winter diet of plain cured ham and seeing such spring greens as cress, onions, and kale heralding spring in the lowlands, combined ham and greens into one glorious dish."

Eugene Smith of St. Mary's County picking beans

Smith canning beans

Today, there is little debate that Stuffed Ham was a creation of the people enslaved by the priests.

Young said, in an oral history, that the dish was devised as a way to use up the pieces of the ham that they'd been given. She described the jaw being boiled with the greens before the priests decided, "Well, it's good! But if we use the good part of the ham, it would be better."

"St. Mary's County Stuffed Ham was probably born of necessity," Bertha's 89-year-old cousin Everlyn Holland once wrote to a local newspaper, "and its origin passed on orally in the slave community."

Easter ham aside, Stuffed Ham has long ago joined the table at Thanksgiving, Christmas, and other celebrations in the region. At some stores, you can get it year-round.

Bertha contends that her ham is not quite as good as that made by her mother, "but it's close."

After she'd chopped her cabbage-heavy blend of greens and seasoned them, I watched as Bertha thoroughly massaged the ingredients together for a good while. I observed that the process breaks down the cabbage in a way that achieves what I do through blanching. With the greens well-macerated, more stuffing can be packed into the slits in the ham.

Whether to blanch or massage the greens isn't the only decision to be made.

Once the corned ham has been rinsed comes the real dilemma – to bone or not to bone? In 1988, Baltimore Sun writer Rob Kasper explored the controversy.

> **"Ham Bone advocates cook the ham with the bone still in it. They argue that the bone gives flavor and posture to a stuffed ham,"** he wrote. But then, **"Anti-bone forces contend that with the bone removed, the ham is easier to slice and 'you can fill up the bone-hole with more stuffing.'"**

This lyrical passage rings in my head when I de-bone a ham.

The choice of greens raises the most possibilities. Cabbage, kale, and mustard are fairly standard; cress is less common. Some old recipes even call for shallot or onion tops.

According to Kasper, "Almost everybody agrees that the best way to enjoy a stuffed ham is to slice it and serve it in sandwiches." The rest of the particulars are enough to make your head spin but that is some advice I am glad to heed.

It takes a lifetime of expertise to coax the perfect flavor out of stuffed ham, but that hasn't stopped me from putting it on the table before my loved ones. I've been happy with the results but I will always be refining it. A stuffed ham recipe should be viewed merely as a starting point toward one's own formula. —KMH

Stuffed Ham

 St. Mary's County  main dish

My goal is to get a delicious, flavorful stuffed ham onto your table without tears. You can do this!

Yields 6–8 servings  turnip & mustard GREENS

QUICK TIP

You will be most likely to find corned ham available for purchase when it is most commonly served—near Christmas. Call ahead. I was able to find deboned corned ham at J W Treuth & Sons' in Catonsville in early December and all of the greens at H Mart, a five minute drive away on Rolling Road. Most butchers get it from Baltimore-based Mangers Meat, which is also open to the public and worth checking out.

This is a Southern Maryland delicacy that even many Marylanders have not had. The trip to St Mary's County is long from most other parts of the state. Luckily you can make it at home with good results. While restaurants down there might make it year-round it's clear it's a cold weather dish. Not only does its use of late fall greens and the use of corned ham sync it up with the winter months—you need time to process the pig and corn the ham—it needs to be cooled before putting it in the refrigerator. The fastest way to do this is to cover and put it outside or on a uninsulated porch on a winter's night. Alternately you could place the pot in a trough or massive cooler filled with ice until cool, but I've never had anything that would be big enough to use.

The trick with the recipe is not getting overwhelmed and using the right ingredients. You might be more familiar with corned beef but corned ham is what is used here. Fresh ham is processed in a brine for many days until it is drained and ready to stuff. You can brine it yourself but I cannot stress how much better and easier it is to procure an already corned ham. It is very difficult to corn fresh ham at home safely. I also recommend buying the corned ham deboned if possible. Some say the bone adds flavor but it is difficult to remove from the ham and removing it gives you more space for stuffing. A deboned ham is also easier to fit in a lobster pot, crab pot, or other very large pot.

Many recipes call for kale and for chopping the ingredients all by hand. I did not find this yielded the best results. The kale was bitter and it took a long time to remove the leaves from the stem. Hand chopping is, of course, a fine option but I found using my food processor and working in batches worked much better to produce a uniform mixture that was easy to stuff into the ham. Unless you truly love chopping and can do it well, get your hands on a food processor and use that.

THE GREENS

- ½ large cabbage
- 1 bunch turnip greens
- 1 bunch mustard greens
- 2 bunches watercress
- 2 long green peppers (or one cubanelle)
- 1 stalk celery
- 1 bunch scallions
- 1 small onion

SEASONINGS

- 3 tablespoons mustard seed
- ½ tablespoon ground mustard
- ½ tablespoon celery seed
- 3 tablespoons hot red pepper flakes (I liked the batch using Korean gochugaru flakes the best but any will work.)

THE HAM

- 1 16-lb corned ham (deboned)

EXTRAS

enough cheesecloth to wrap around the ham multiple times

kitchen twine

DIRECTIONS:

Work in batches to process all of the vegetables in a food processor to uniformly chop them. You don't want to make paste (or pesto!) but you want them like you would have in a fine coleslaw.

I removed the thickest bits of the stem from the **mustard and turnip greens** before tearing them into pieces to put in the food processor. The **watercress** does not have tough stems so you can just separate it out into bunches to process.

I processed the **pepper, celery** and both **onions** together.

After each batch, I added it to a very large bowl and stirred. Once all of the raw vegetables were processed, I added the **seasonings** and stirred to evenly distribute everything.

Put the vegetables aside and unwrap the ham.

It will be very large, floppy and wide. I used two big cutting boards side by side and placed the **ham** on top. I cut deep slits (about 2 inches deep) all around the **ham** using a very sharp knife. Take your time! It is slippery. I stuffed those slits and the parts where the bone had been with the filling. I just kept making slits and stuffing **the greens** in there until I ran out of greens. **The greens** do leach a bit of liquid as you are doing this, be prepared. Ideally, I would do this outside on a picnic table or in an industrial kitchen that can be hosed down but two massive cutting boards worked well enough. Roll the **ham** closed and wrap in kitchen twine any direction you have to to keep it closed. This is not time to worry about aesthetics. Wrap it in the cheese cloth and with more twine.

Fill a large pot with water—use a lobster or crab pot, any pot that will fit and fully cover the **ham**. Lower the ham into it. Make sure it is covered in water. You can add any leaked filling into the water if you'd like or additional spices.

Cook for 15 minutes per pound, adding more hot water as needed. As it cooks it will shrink and you can sort of roll it around in there to make sure it is evenly cooking. The temperature needs to reach 160° for 2 minutes. Check repeatedly in different areas of the **ham** using a probe thermometer.

Cool in the liquid as quickly as you can. As mentioned in the tip, I placed it on my below freezing porch for almost 2 hours. It needs to be cool enough to be refrigerated within 2 hours. Drain the **ham**. Place in a large container or back in the same (cleaned) pot and refrigerate overnight.

Unwrap and slice.

Traditionally it's served cold. Sandwiches are popular. We really enjoyed the leftovers made into fried rice.

HOLIDAY TRADITIONS FROM THE OLD LINE STATE

SAUERKRAUT
for Thanksgiving

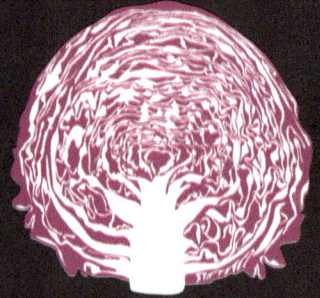  

Sauerkraut came to Baltimore with German (and later, Eastern European) immigrants, but it made the leap to the dinner tables of Baltimore's other citizens, in particular alongside the Thanksgiving turkey.

  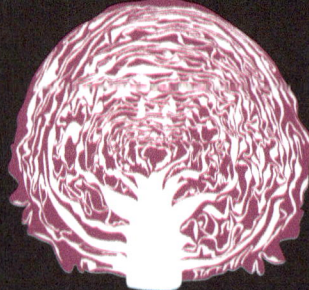

Much has been written about this peculiar phenomenon, including a 2020 piece for the travel website Matador Network in which Rachel was interviewed. She explained how she didn't realize the custom was a local one until she went to college. "People from out of state seemed confused. I thought they were clearly missing out."

Call it the "sauerkraut moment." Chef Tonya Thomas of H3irloom Food Group had a similar experience, going to college in New York to find her peers didn't eat sauerkraut at Thanksgiving.

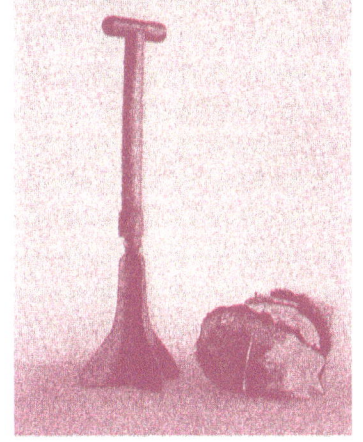

In many places where sauerkraut is eaten, it is stewed with meat cuts or sausages for extra flavor. This was a good fit for Black home cooks' practice of using every part of an animal, and Tonya's grandmother cooked hers with pig tails. Tonya eventually began to flavor her own sauerkraut with smoked turkey instead of pork. More recently, she has flavored the sauerkraut with vegetable stock and spices instead of meat, to accomodate H3irloom's vegan guests.

The formula for sauerkraut itself is so simple that only a handful of recipes appear across my Maryland cookbook collection. It's also long been available for sale in prepared form.

> **"No matter who you are and what your race, in Baltimore, sauerkraut is on the table at holidays,"** Thomas told me.

She can trace the sauerkraut tradition in her family back for generations, to well before the 20th century. When Abraham Lincoln declared Thanksgiving a national holiday in 1863, Germans were the largest group of immigrants in Baltimore, she noted.

In Elizabeth Ellicott Lea's 1845 cookbook "Domestic Cookery," the two recipes for sauerkraut are labeled as "cabbage," suggesting that sauerkraut may have been the primary use for cabbage in her household.

The earliest Maryland recipe calling the dish by name is in the 1870 "Queen of the Kitchen," by Mary Lloyd Tyson. Had Tyson wanted to, she could have purchased prepared sauerkraut at William Bodmann's Pickling House and Vinegar Depot on Howard Street.

In 1886, the Baltimore County Union paper wrote that sauerkraut, "instead of being tabooed, as formerly, had become quite a favorite dish upon our most fashionable tables."

Holiday sauerkraut could be found wherever German people had settled in Maryland. Ads in Frederick newspapers promoted Thanksgiving specials including oysters, cranberries, turkeys, and sauerkraut. A 1930 ad in the Hagerstown Daily Mail touted homemade mince meat and sauerkraut in late November.

Nobody knows just how or why sauerkraut became so cross-cultural in Baltimore in particular.

Christmastime ads for sauerkraut appeared in the Afro-American by 1916. In 1933, they printed a recipe to make your own at home.

Mercedes V. Rankin, one of the first female officers in the Baltimore City Police Department, contributed her sauerkraut recipe to the "Bethel Cookbook," produced in 1979 by the historic Bethel African Methodist Episcopal Church.

Mercedes V. Rankin

A resurgence in the popularity of fermented foods has brought the old custom back to the forefront. In 2022, Baltimore Magazine reported on Krautfest, an annual celebration of all things sauerkraut held at Gertrude's Restaurant. Owner-chef John Shields recalled it being a ubiquitous side-dish during his Baltimore youth, even in Italian neighbors' households, served alongside ravioli and turkey on Thanksgiving. It would be bad luck not to eat "at least a tablespoon," he told the magazine.

The wide adoption across ethnicities, races, and classes has given sauerkraut staying power on holiday tables. Acidic, fermented cabbage is a natural accompaniment to a succulent turkey, not to mention other rich holiday side dishes. Certainly "Francois," a (presumably French) head waiter at Hotel Belvedere in 1921, agreed. He told the Baltimore Sun: "turkey without sauerkraut is like terrapin without champagne." —KMH

Making Sauerkraut, Virginia

 Baltimore City

FERMENTATION

 side dish — Yields 3 cups

INGREDIENTS:

- **7** cups finely shredded cabbage (about 1 very large cabbage)
- **4-5** teaspoons sea salt
- **2** teaspoons mustard seeds

Sauerkraut

Sauerkraut is a great "first fermentation" project anyone can make. It only uses a few ingredients and requires minimal involvement from you. The biggest tips I can give are to make sure everything is very clean from your hands to the cabbage to containers, to avoid any bad bacteria sneaking in and keeping the cabbage submerged and covered. I do this by placing a clean plate that's slightly smaller than the top of the jar or crock on the cabbage topped with a reusable bag full of water. Alternately you can also weigh it down with a bag or jar of rice or beans, or use a very heavy teapot or other clean kitchen item. You may need to add things to the plate to weigh it down more as the cabbage ferments. —RR

DIRECTIONS:

Mix all ingredients together in a large bowl until the cabbage starts to leak water.

Place in a large, nonreactive container like a pickling crock or wide mouth half-gallon jar. **Pack the cabbage** in the container tightly.

There should be enough liquid leached from the cabbage to cover the cabbage. If not, pour in a mixture made of 16 oz water and 1 tablespoon sea salt until it is covered.

Weigh down the cabbage with a plate or shallow, wide bowl topped with a heavy object like a water filled bag. You want to keep the cabbage below the liquid line.

Allow to ferment in a cool, dry place for at least **1 week**. Check it daily and skim off any scum that may float to the top. You may not get any scum but if you do, it needs to be removed. It should look and taste like sauerkraut when it's ready! The smaller the container, the quicker it will ferment.

After fermenting, refrigerate in an airtight container for up to 6 months.

Mrs. Percy Duvall's
TURKEY STUFFED WITH OYSTERS

"Think How Much We Can Be Thankful For," declared a column by Jerome P. Fleishman in the Baltimore Sun. It was November 22, 1914. "Peace and plenty here while Europe is bleeding" was the subtitle. In Baltimore, the grain ports were bustling. The article's figurative "optimist" character speculated that our country would prosper from replenishing the war-torn continent's supplies. News of the war ran below the fold. Above it, the main attraction was a full-sized cartoon of a family chasing a turkey, entitled "They're Rounding Up the Old Gobbler Down Home."

The war was vying for the attention of Baltimore, but it wasn't winning out over Thanksgiving.

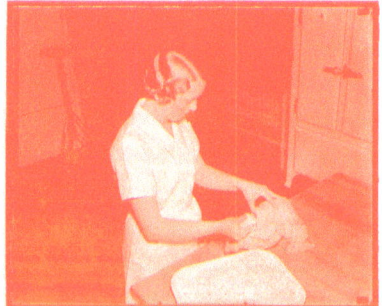

On the second page, the paper reported the planned meals of President Wilson, Baltimore's Mayor Preston, socialite Walter de Curzon Poultney, and Sheriff Thomas McNulty. The mayor would be having sauerkraut, Cape Cod cranberries, and broiled sweet potatoes. Poultney would be having stewed potatoes, plum pudding, and Harford County cider. The Sheriff's wife said "he can't seem to see anything on the table except the sauerkraut— that is, until he comes to the mince pies." All of these men, including the president, would also be having turkey— turkey stuffed with oysters.

The practice of stuffing meats with oysters wasn't always reserved for turkey. Many old recipes for beef à la mode featured a filling made with oysters, breadcrumbs, and herbs. Anchovy was another common ingredient in these dishes, but near the Chesapeake, oysters were the obvious choice for adding a briny depth of flavor to savory meats. Beef à la mode may have fallen out of fashion, but oyster stuffing for turkey gained staying power, perhaps from Thanksgiving's tendency to etch certain traditions into stone.

Some of the oldest Maryland cookbooks contain recipes for turkey served with oysters. In her 1870 book "Queen of the Kitchen," Mary Lloyd Tyson, a relative of Frances Scott Key, suggested a casserole of sorts, with cooked turkey and oysters layered and topped with breadcrumbs.

Later books incorporated oysters into stuffing or 'dressing' for turkey. George Forbes of Baltimore collected recipes from Maryland and Virginia families and packaged them into a novelty box of "Colonial Cook Cards" in 1907. The cards and the box contained imagery of a southern belle holding a fan in one hand, with a "Mammy" figure standing at attention. (The recipe card set is one example of the early 20th-century tendency to use the word "colonial" as a euphemism for antebellum.) One recipe, from the Waring family of Prince George's County, called for "12 or more" oysters mixed into a dressing and then sewn into a turkey which was subsequently boiled. The dressing was flavored only with nutmeg, a possible indication that the recipe may indeed date to colonial times.

Many oyster stuffing recipes are for a turkey cooked with the stuffing inside it - a practice now considered to be inadvisable because of the risk of salmonella. "When a long tined fork thrust in the fleshy part of the thigh shall not be followed by a watery ooze of pinkish color, the turkey is quite cooked," wrote Mrs. Percy Duvall in the 1920 "Melwood Cookbook".

Old, vague directions like these can be charming until you turn from the cookbooks to the newspapers and find stories of sickness and death from "ptomaine poisoning." If you serve this stuffing for Thanksgiving, you can be thankful for thermometers and food safety.

Mrs. Duvall's recipe combined mushrooms, oysters, and ham in a stuffing made with stale biscuits or "bakers bread." "Season highly," she recommended; "great care must be taken that the oysters are not cooked. They should be hot, not cooked, before they are taken from the fire."

Oyster Stuffing

Prince George's County — 9

white bread and OYSTERS

Yields 8 servings | side dish

Chesapeake oyster stuffing is normally made with white bread, unlike the cornbread-based oyster stuffing you find in other oyster-rich areas. While I like cornbread, I do find using a milder, more finely crumbed bread lets the oysters really shine.

Traditionally, you would stuff a raw turkey with an oyster-rich filling but modern-day health guidelines warn against that as it is difficult to reach and maintain a safe temperature for both the turkey and the stuffing. After some experimentation, I found the texture and flavor was best and most consistent when it was baked separately in its own dish.

Technically I would call this a dressing since it is made outside of the turkey or chicken, but out of respect for the original recipe and the observed tendency of Marylanders not to differentiate between the two, I will call it stuffing.

Older recipes call for you to use stale biscuits, a welcome and thrifty tip because as we all know biscuits only last a day or two before they are too dry and unappetizing to eat as-is. I kept that spirit and used a variety of stale bread goods in my stuffing. I found I liked a combination of stale brioche hamburger buns and a couple of slices of white sandwich bread the most, but any slightly stale bread would work—there is no reason to buy bread, especially for this recipe, you are spending enough already on the oysters. I similarly used leftover ham, another traditional ingredient, which adds a nice smoky flavor to the stuffing but if you have it, tasso ham is also very good. —RR

Alongside its 1914 reports on the Thanksgiving dinners of the various prominent men, the Baltimore Sun ran some "tested recipes" for oyster stuffing and pumpkin pie, and the advice: "If you are living south of the Mason and Dixon line and inside the oyster belt at Thanksgiving time it is nothing short of heresy to fail to serve turkey with good old-fashioned oyster stuffing, just as it has been prepared in Maryland since time out o'mind."

With similar confidence, the "optimist" column in that day's paper assured readers, "[President Wilson] kept us out of trouble in Mexico, and he's going to keep us out of trouble across seas! So long as a man minds his own business, works hard, and thinks cheerful thoughts, he's safe. It's the same way with a nation. Now, let's go to church Thanksgiving's Day and appreciate our blessings. What do you say?" —**KMH**

INGREDIENTS:

- 2 stalks celery (with greens), diced
- 1 large onion, diced
- 1 pint shucked oysters, with liquor
- 6 cups loosely torn slightly stale white bread or rolls
- 2 eggs, at room temperature
- ⅓ cup diced ham (I used leftover spiral sliced ham)
- ¼-½ teaspoon celery seed
- ½ teaspoon dried thyme
- ½ teaspoon dried savory
- ½ teaspoon dried marjoram
- salt
- freshly ground black pepper

DIRECTIONS:

Preheat oven to 350. Butter a 8x8 inch baking dish, set aside.

In a large pan, melt some **butter** and sauté the **celery** and **onions** until the celery is tender and the onions are translucent, about 15 minutes. Add the **oysters and the liquor** and cook for 30 seconds.

While the celery and onions are cooking, place the **bread**, **eggs**, **ham**, and **spices** in a large bowl and stir to evenly distribute all the ingredients.

When the oyster mixture is ready, add to the bread and stir to evenly distribute the ingredients again. Spoon into the prepared pan.

Cover with foil and bake 20 minutes. Remove foil and bake 5-10 additional minutes or until the stuffing is cooked through but slightly creamy-custardy in the middle and the top is lightly crispy.

Serve immediately.

This dish is best the day it is made but you can refrigerate the leftovers for up to two days. I like to let it sit out for about 10 minutes before heating it up in the oven.

If your celery does not have greens attached, sub in about ¼ (loose) cup flat leaf parsley leaves.

APPLE TODDY

"If the recrudescence of apple toddy depends on you, then it will not recrudesce, you determine, and so when someone says, 'Let's make eggnog instead,' you drop the half-dozen apples to which you have been holding desperately and join with the unimaginative, mediocre, conventional crowd that always does the obvious thing." – "Christmas Echoes, With The Story of The Forgotten Recipe For An Insidious Drink", Baltimore Sun, December 1911.

From the late 18th through the early 20th centuries, when the winter holiday season came around in Maryland and huge bowls of libations were put out for traveling guests, eggnog was not the only game in town.

It was an old adage that "cobwebs on the demijohn" authenticated an apple toddy of the best quality, with some recipes calling for an entire year of aging. The relative hassle and patience-testing of preparing a beverage a year in advance could be to blame for the decline in popularity of Apple Toddy. Perhaps it was the decline in the availability of Maryland Rye. Once a booming industry and a point of state pride, Maryland Rye production never recovered after Prohibition, and distilleries closed for good.

Then again, some recipes don't even contain rye. The combination of liquors used in apple toddy varies wildly. Some contain champagne or Curaçao. Brandy is pretty standard.

Even the treatment of the apples is up for debate. Annapolitan Louis Dorsey Gassaway's (1862-1940) recipe in "Maryland's Way: The Hammond-Harwood House Cookbook" instructs one to stud apples with cloves and bake them before leaving them immersed, whole, in the liquors for a year. A recipe found in the c.1869 Hall Family Papers Cookbook at the Maryland Center for History and Culture advises instead straining the apple pulp into the booze. This is much more work but results in a more flavorful toddy.

You may want to steer clear of artificially flavored brandies. And make sure to dilute the final product in order to further your enjoyment and lessen your hangover. —KMH

DIRECTIONS:

Slice apples and stick with cloves. Roast at 375° until apples begin to brown and wrinkle. Cover apples with liquors, adding lemon peel if desired. Let stand at least four hours before straining (pressing the apples). Heat some of the water, dissolve sugar in it, and combine with strained toddy to serve, hot or cold.

½ cup peach brandy
(or apricot brandy)

½ cup Jamaica rum

lemon rind
(if desired)

6 apples
(preferably Stayman or Winesap)

1-2 quarts water

2 cups Whiskey
(Maryland Rye preferred)

4-6 cloves

½ cup sugar
(or to taste)

HOLIDAY TRADITIONS FROM THE OLD LINE STATE

Thanksgiving
WHITE POTATO PIES

A Baltimore Sun correspondent from Ellicott's Mills wrote on December 1st, 1843, the day after that year's Thanksgiving, that "it is said that pumpkin pie will make a Yankee's mouth water. Be that as it may; but give me good fat turkey and pumpkin pie… that pie! O, that pumpkin pie! Who can properly express the deliciousness of that pumpkin pie?"

Tastes change. In 1907 the Sun had done a turnabout on pumpkin pie, printing an editorial that declared it to be "a vile pretender" which was "tolerated, but not loved." The author lamented that pumpkin pie was just a vehicle for spices and declared that "examined in the cold glare of actual fact, the pumpkin pie becomes obviously bogus and unspeakably contemptible."

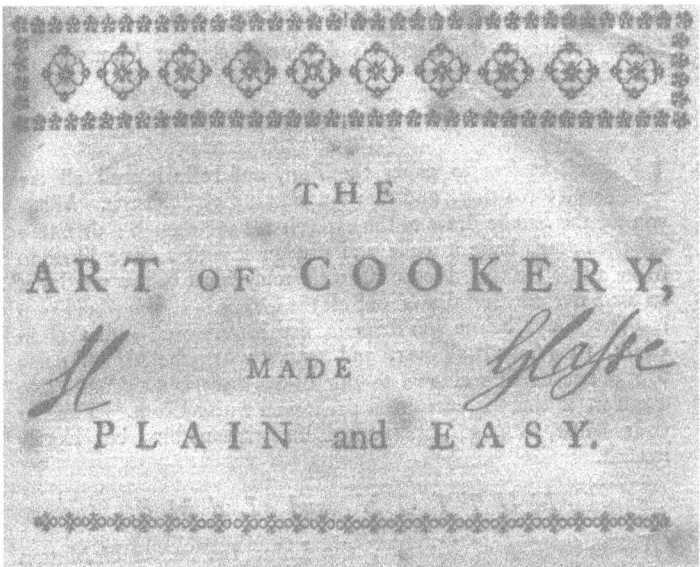

What on earth happened? Well, for starters there are the very Northern "Yankee" associations of pumpkin pie in a state whose loyalties had been torn apart in the Civil War. Historian David Shields has pointed to the widespread availability of canned pumpkin. "Canned pumpkin pie filling from the North and its distribution through southern groceries set off the woe reflex in southerners," wrote Shields. Pumpkin pie and its Southern counterpart, the sweet potato pie, became symbolic. The perceived replacement of the latter by the former aroused anxieties about fading traditions and culture.

Today, the "vile pretender" finds a home on many a Maryland Thanksgiving table, although sweet-potato pie lovers often shake a rueful head at pumpkin pie. In many cases, the preference is determined by race, with sweet potato pie standing as a pillar of the soul food canon.

Old Line Plate will take no stance on this matter, instead offering a recipe for the wild card option: White Potato Pie.

Like sweet potato and pumpkin pies, white potato pie is the descendent of "pudding" made from squashes, carrots, or potatoes, sweetened and flavored with nutmeg and/or lemon.

Hannah Glasse's white potato pudding recipes are some of the oldest recorded. In her 1774 book "The Art of Cookery," she included three variations for 'potato pudding'. Only the third explicitly specified 'white' potatoes. That recipe remains nearly identical to modern ones – enriched with cream, butter, and eggs; flavored with nutmeg and wine; baked in a "puff paste." She suggested decorating the pie with citron or orange peel.

Mary Randolph's 1824 cookbook "The Virginia House-Wife" took the pie down a notch – it is included as a mere afterthought. Sweet potato pudding, she wrote, can be made by flavoring mashed sweet potatoes with nutmeg, lemon peel, and brandy, cooked in a pastry and decorated with citron. "Irish potato pudding is made in the same manner," she noted, "but is not so good."

Despite this not-so-ringing endorsement, white potato pie/pudding persisted. Recipes can be found in handwritten recipe manuscripts, classic Maryland cookbooks like Mary Lloyd Tyson's 1870 "Queen of the Kitchen," and community cookbooks spanning the 19th and 20th centuries.

When Virginian Ruth Gaskins included white potato pie in her 1968 cookbook "A Good Heart and A Light Hand," it captured imaginations. Associated Press food editor Cecily Brownstone prominently featured the recipe in an article about soul food cookbooks. Newspapers across the country ran the article in July of 1969. "White Potato Pie: It's Soul Food," declared a headline in the Santa Cruz Sentinel. By August that year, a flurry of requests prompted Baltimore Evening Sun food columnist Virginia Roeder to publish several more recipes for white potato pie.

How this pie became associated with Maryland is a bit of a mystery. One possibility is that the confusion with the Eastern Shore's beloved White Hayman sweet potatoes is partially to blame. Another less tangible answer may be social networks – the ways recipes have been shared and propagated through families, churches, and communities.

White Potato Pie got a big boost from All Hallows Church in Davidsonville. The church included a white potato pie in their annual Thanksgiving dinner, a cherished parish tradition that started around 1900. The church shared its recipe in the 1966 "Maryland's Way" cookbook benefitting the Hammond-Harwood house in Annapolis. Interests were piqued and the recipe appeared in news stories about the cookbook. 'Maryland-ness' began to be burnished into the very idea of White Potato Pie.

It was probably Oxmoor House that sealed the deal. When they adapted recipes from "Maryland's Way" into their "Southern Heritage Cookbook Library" series, the company's editors frequently added "Maryland" to the name. Thus, in 1983, white potato pie officially became "Maryland White Potato Pie," both in the cookbooks and in Oxmoor House's Southern Living and Good Housekeeping magazines.

After speaking engagements, I'm often asked about white potato pie. It sounds so strange to some people. A few others have shared memories of the pie being served in their families. When I was profiled in the Baltimore Sun in 2019, I knew just which recipe to highlight. I've grown to love White Potato Pie and the way it has connected me with readers.

Despite the amount of press and intrigue surrounding this humble, custardy fall pie, white potato pie doesn't seem to be experiencing a resurgence. It's the compromise no one asked for. Whether you're a fan of the juicy flavor of pumpkin, or the velvet texture of sweet potato, White Potato Pie only demands an appreciation of the flavor of lemon and a sense of adventure. —KMH

Farm and Home Show, Salisbury, 1968

White Potato Pie

Anne Arundel County	Yields one 8 inch pie		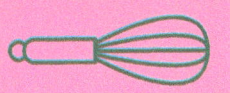	sweet dish

The trick to an excellent white potato pie is beaten egg whites. It is one more step and it can seem scary when it comes time to fold them into the potato mixture, but I assure you it is worth it. It elevates the humble potato into something that is that is truly holiday-worthy by giving the pie a creamy yet light texture. —RR

INGREDIENTS:

- 1 unbaked single layer pie crust (use store-bought refrigerated or your favorite homemade recipe)
- 2 lbs Russet potatoes, peeled, roughly chopped and boiled until fork-tender (about 4 cups chopped, cooked potatoes)
- 1 cup sugar, divided use
- 3 eggs, divided use
- ⅓ cup butter, melted and cooled slightly
- 1 teaspoon vanilla
- ¾ cup heavy cream
- 1 teaspoon freshly grated nutmeg
- ½ teaspoon ground mace
- juice and zest of one lemon

DIRECTIONS:

Preheat oven to **375°**.

Place the **pie crust** in the bottom of a pie plate. Prick with a fork and pre-bake for 8 minutes. Set aside.

In a large bowl or bowl of a stand mixer, mash the **potatoes**. Add the **¾ cup sugar**, **egg yolks**, **butter**, **vanilla**, **cream**, **nutmeg**, **mace**, and the **lemon juice and zest**. Mix until a fairly smooth batter forms. Set aside.

In a second bowl, beat the **egg whites** with the whisk attachment until frothy and white. While the mixer is running, slowly stream in the **remaining ¼ cup sugar** and continue to beat until stiff peaks form—when you lift the whisk, the egg should hold its shape and not double back down on itself.

Use a spoon to fold the whites into the potato batter, carefully spooning batter over the whites so as not to deflate them. It might be a little lumpy looking but that's okay.

Pour into the prepared pie crust. You don't want it to spill over the sides, but it should be level to the top of the pie plate or even slightly mounded above.

Sprinkle with more **nutmeg** if desired.

Bake for **50 minutes** or until lightly browned and set in the middle.

Cool completely on a wire rack before slicing and serving.

Maryland
PLUM PUDDING

"When we were children the making of Christmas plum pudding was quite a ceremony. The fruits were prepared, the whole family helped to cut the suet fine, and everyone, from father to the baby, had a hand in stirring it."
- Mrs. Mary Morton,
The Hagerstown Daily Mail, 1937

In 1889, the Washington, DC Evening Star printed a recipe for "A Maryland Plum Pudding warranted to keep a year," made with staggering quantities including six pounds of raisins, six pounds of brown sugar, four pounds of currants, six pounds of "stale oated bread," six pounds of eggs, six pounds of suet, two pounds of citron, and three nutmegs. The recipe contained a mere half pint each of brandy and wine and "a little mace." (Like most plum puddings, it contained zero plums.) After being boiled for four hours, the pudding was exposed to the sun for two or three days "with the cloth on" and hung to dry in a cold room.

This is one of the few recipes that I know of for an explicitly-named "Maryland" plum pudding, but then most of my recipes come from within the state; perhaps there was less impulse to namedrop one's own home. On the other hand, that didn't discourage everyone. A 1906 Christmas luncheon given by the Baltimore Merchants' Club featured "old Virginia apple toddy, Maryland plum pudding, Maryland eggnog, Virginia ham, and Maryland biscuits." Provenance creates prestige, and plum pudding was no exception.

When recipes for plum pudding were printed in newspapers in the 1800s, they already had an air of nostalgia for times gone by. Many of the recipes claimed to originate in the Colonial period or even earlier, when it's said "plum" could refer to any type of dried fruit.

One recipe found in Frederick Philip Stieff's 1932 book "Eat, Drink & Be Merry in Maryland" is entitled "Ellin North Plum Pudding," and claims to have belonged to "the first white child born in Baltimore" in 1740.

A recipe found in the 1907 book "Colonial Recipes, From Old Virginia and Maryland Manors, with Numerous Legends and Traditions Interwoven" by Maude A. Bomberger (who can take credit for that doozy of a title as well) is linked to Isabel S. Mason, lineal descendent of the Randolph family, "of King Robert Bruce of Scotland."

Sometimes these stories can be dubious, but plum pudding is an ancient English tradition and nothing in its ingredients screams out

"Plum Pudding" Self-Saucing Pudding Cake

Turning plum pudding into something that people can both easily make (no pudding mold or suet required) and want to make this century was a journey. I was having pudding-related nightmares and waking up in a dried fruit-related panic.

Finally, I had the idea to combine the flavors and most of the ingredients of a traditional steamed pudding with the technique of another type of "pudding" (none of this is pudding in the American sense) that is popular in Australia: the self-saucing pudding. It yields a texture that is surprisingly similar to traditional plum pudding. This is thanks to the unusual technique of pouring very hot water over the dry cake ingredients and then baking it until the cake rises through the liquid leaving a layer of caramel or sauce below, effectively steaming the cake in the oven. The result is a layer of soft spiced cake studded with fruit over a layer of molasses-caramel. —RR

Maryland. Yields 8 servings. Soft spiced cake studded with fruit over a layer of molasses-caramel. sweet dish

MARYLAND PLUM PUDDING.

Two cupfuls bread crumbs, one cupful flour, one cupful raisins, one cupful currants, one cupful suet, one cupful molasses, one wineglassful of brandy, one half cupful of citron, three eggs, one teaspoonful cloves, two teaspoonfuls cinnamon. Steam four hours. Serve with hard brandy sauce.

Mrs. H. D. Ingraham.

'progress,' so there may be truth to these claims. Not to mention, recipes that get pulled out religiously once a year tend to be preserved. Plum pudding used to be so mandatory for Thanksgiving and Christmas that it was an idiom: **"Christmas without plum pudding is like a sky without stars,"** according to an 1888 advertisement in the Baltimore Sun.

FOR THE CAKE LAYER:

- 1 cup dried fruit (I used a combination of raisins, Zante currants, dried Montmorency cherries, candied citron, and candied orange peel)
- Zest and juice of one orange (about ½ cup juice)
- 1½ cups flour
- 1½ teaspoons baking powder
- ½ teaspoon cinnamon
- ½ teaspoon nutmeg
- ¼ teaspoon mace
- ¼ teaspoon cloves
- 2 tablespoons butter, melted and cooled slightly
- ½ cup heavy cream
- ½ cup granulated sugar

FOR THE SAUCE LAYER:

- 6 tablespoons butter
- 2 cups water
- ½ cup light brown sugar
- 1 tablespoon vanilla
- 1½ tablespoons blackstrap unsulfured molasses

DIRECTIONS:

Preheat oven to **375°**. Butter a 2 ½ quart baking dish—you want one with fairly tall sides, not a shallow cake tin or pie plate.

While the oven preheats, soak the **dried fruit** in the **orange juice and zest** (about 10 minutes) in a small bowl or measuring cup.

Place the fruit and the rest of the cake ingredients in a large bowl and stir to evenly distribute all the ingredients. The mixture will be fairly dry and lumpy.

Pour the mixture into the prepared pan.

In small saucepan, heat all **sauce ingredients** together, whisking occasionally to dissolve the sugar, until it just begins to boil. Carefully pour evenly over the cake mixture in the pan.

Bake for **50 minutes** or until the top looks dry and "set".

Cool on wire rack about 5 minutes before serving warm.

Good with vanilla ice cream.

At the turn of the 20th century, cooks and newspapers began to adapt and revamp plum pudding with varieties suiting modern kitchens, budgets, and (especially) tastes. These recipes were usually printed alongside traditional or "English" versions. In 1936, the Evening Sun declared "a very modern adaptation" with chocolate and gelatin to be "surprisingly good." Flaming brandy was swapped out with whipped cream. Another year, the Evening Sun printed a recipe that was suited for "1932 pocketbooks."

Despite these updates, plum pudding began to die a slow death. The increasing availability of pre-packaged puddings didn't help. Perhaps it even hurt. It was once believed that every family member should stir the pudding for good luck, but does good luck fit into a can?

Huge recipe quantities were meant for gifting, but is the gift special if your friends can buy a reasonable amount of plum pudding off the grocery shelf?

Writer Francis F. Beirne, under the pen name of Christopher Billopp, took to the pages of the Evening Sun in 1953 to sing the praises of plum pudding and express anxieties about its future: "In every generation of a family there is one member who is the guardian of the plum-pudding recipe. Around Christmas time that member is foremost in importance.

… The younger generation will show little interest in the recital of the virtues of the plum pudding… the most crushing blow of all comes when they confess they don't really like plum pudding and would much rather have ice cream instead."

If Beirne had had his way, parents would "not give in to such whims. They should tell their children they have got to eat plum pudding. Even if they take only a mouthful of it."

By 1981, plum pudding had become a punchline. Elsie T. Chisholm wrote a column in the Evening Sun about an uneaten plum pudding that had made the rounds in her family for years. "Plum pudding," she wrote, was like "sauerkraut and turkey. It's a custom, but not a custom everyone has to follow."

The Baltimore Sun last printed a plum pudding recipe in 2002, entitling it "Scrooge's Plum Pudding." For years beforehand, columns mentioning plum pudding no longer recalled Maryland's Christmases past, as they once had. The focus instead was squarely on plum pudding's English roots.

Beirne disagreed. For him, a distaste for plum pudding was downright unpatriotic. "No plum pudding?… The country is degenerating, that's what it is," he wrote. For children to say they don't want any of the plum pudding, "they might as well refuse to salute the flag." —**KMH**

Christmas
OYSTER STEW

Oystermen of Baltimore

"A century ago in old New England and New York a bowl of piping hot oyster stew formed the traditional Christmas Eve supper, now practiced only by a few families who have preserved the tradition along with grandmother's Chippendale and pewter… The homemakers of today would do well to revive this custom for the oyster has a happy way of inducing sleep of the deep and restful kind. Then too, it is easy to prepare, requires no expensive ingredients, no left overs striving for a corner in a refrigerator filled with Christmas foods. And then too, the ease with which the stew is digested may well prepare you to do justice to that Christmas dinner." – Denton Journal, 1937

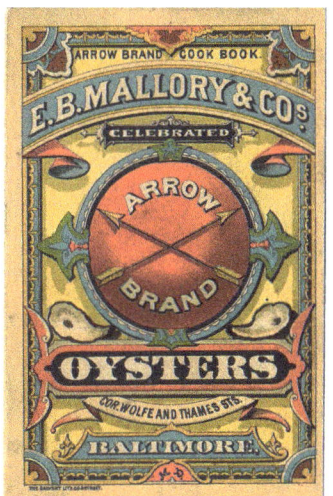

There was a time when Oyster Stew for Christmas seemed to be as old a tradition as plum pudding, but that was not actually the case. Oyster Stew only came about in the United States in the 1840s, with Catholic Irish immigrants who abstained from meat on Christmas Eve. Locally abundant oysters took the place of fish and quickly became the standard.

And why not? Oyster Stew is an easy option for those looking to revive a lost custom. It is one of the most frequently-occurring recipes in the Old Line Plate database. And variations come down to just a few ingredients.

Mrs. Benjamin Chew Howard included five recipes "to stew oysters" in "Fifty Years in a Maryland Kitchen," her influential 1873 cookbook. They vary in complexity. One recipe, a single sentence long, contained five gallons of oysters, half an onion, and three tablespoons of ginger. Another contained mustard, cayenne pepper, walnut catsup, and Worcestershire sauce.

A recipe in a 1948 cookbook entitled "A Cook's Tour of the Eastern Shore" is one of the few bearing Christmas in the name. Recipe contributor Edith Adkins advised oysters cooked

> *"If one is slowly becoming a Marylander, one is learning to serve oyster stew on Christmas and sauerkraut with one's turkey,"*
> – The Baltimore Sun, 1978

An 1890 housekeeping guide, "Home Dissertations," published by Baltimore importers and grocers Hopper and McGaw, provided some advice: "When canned oysters are used, which is generally the case away from the sea-coast, do not use the liquor, but if fresh oysters can be had the liquor should always be used."

In "300 Years of Black Cooking in St. Mary's County," Theresa Young suggested thickening the stew with a roux made with Tabasco sauce. In that same book, Russell Causby instructed: "heat to boiling without boiling."

in their liquor, with celery, evaporated milk, and whole milk, seasoned with nutmeg, cloves, pepper, and salt.

In 1987, the Evening Sun encouraged a comeback of Oyster Stew for Christmas. "For starters, oyster stew is simplicity itself to make on that night when no one has time or inclination for cooking," wrote columnist Frances Price. And it is true, oyster stew is simple - once you can make up your mind how to make yours. Ultimately, you have to follow your tastes where they lead you. No point in reviving a tradition if you don't make it personal. —KMH

Oyster Stew

Talbot County
cubanelle pepper

Yields 4 servings

main dish

MILK

What Marylanders call oyster "stew" is close to what other areas might call a chowder; it's more than just oysters and cream, it has potatoes and vegetables. There is an annual chowder contest in St. Michaels, Maryland where attendees can taste and vote on the best stew. I've kept it simple but I've had variations that drift towards Maryland crab soup territory and include carrots and lima beans. The beauty of the stew is that you can customize it to your taste.

In this recipe, I'm giving you the choice of using evaporated milk or half and half. Honestly, I prefer evaporated milk. It is very creamy without the heaviness of cream and since it's been heated during the canning process, I find it when I use it the stew is less likely to split. You can also use a mix of 50% half and half and 50% evaporated milk. I know it can seem odd to use canned milk in a luxurious recipe but to me, it works and doesn't have a "canned" flavor but I know that some people will prefer an even more decadent stew and will want to use the half and half. —RR

INGREDIENTS:

- 2 tablespoons butter or olive oil
- 1 large onion, diced
- 1 large russet potato, diced
- 2 stalks celery (with greens attached), diced
- 2 cloves garlic, minced
- 1 cubanelle pepper, chopped
- 1 cup diced smoked ham
- 24 oz evaporated milk (or half and half)
- 1 cup milk
- 1 lb oysters with liquor
- ½ teaspoon celery seed
- salt
- pepper

DIRECTIONS:

Heat the **butter or oil** in a Dutch oven or large pot. Add the **onion**, **potato**, **celery**, **garlic**, **pepper** and **ham** and continue to sauté over low heat until the vegetables are softened and the onion is translucent.

Add the remaining ingredients and simmer until the liquid is hot but not boiling, about 10-15 minutes. Add the **oysters** and continue simmering until the oysters are cooked through, about 5 minutes.

The trick to flavorful oyster stew is to have a good bit of oyster liquor in the broth. Don't get carried away and drain your oysters! If you are lucky, the fish monger might be willing to part with a little extra just for you to add to your stew.

HOLIDAY TRADITIONS FROM THE OLD LINE STATE

WASSAIL BOWL (ALCOHOL-FREE)

In the mid-1800s, Erastus Snow traveled more of the country than many of us will in a lifetime. After converting in 1832 to Mormonism (what is now The Church of Jesus Christ of Latter-day Saints), Snow dedicated his life to spreading the church (and colonizing the Southwest). One online biography of Snow refers to him as a "Faithful servant, missionary, and colonizer."

Somewhere along the way, Snow and three other missionaries stopped near Hagerstown, Maryland, and established the Mormon church there in 1837. Snow is said to have engaged in a debate with a local preacher from two in the afternoon until midnight, inspiring the immediate baptism of nearly 20 converts. Snow would go on to settle in the Salt Lake Valley in 1847.

Today, roughly 1% of Marylanders identify as LDS Church members. Their presence is made known in the D.C. area by the Mormon temple, visible from the Capital Beltway, but there are congregations (known as wards) in other parts of the state.

Members of the LDS Church are taught to abstain from alcohol and caffeinated beverages, so I turned to my LDS cookbooks for a non-alcoholic beverage option, which is often lacking at holiday parties. I have two books, one from the early 1980s, produced by the Hampstead Ward in the Baltimore area, and a 1975 book from the Hagerstown Branch. Both contained similar recipes for this alcohol-free take on Wassail, a spiced cider dating to ancient times. The version in the Hagerstown book, with festive clove-studded oranges, was contributed by Sharon Sanders. The wassail, like the LDS Church itself, is an example of ancient traditions changing over time. —KMH

- 1 teaspoon lemon rind
- 6 cups apple cider (or juice)
- ¼ cup honey
- ¼ teaspoon nutmeg
- 1 cinnamon stick
- 3 tablespoon lemon juice
- 3 whole oranges
- whole cloves
- 1 can unsweetened pineapple juice (2-½ cups)

DIRECTIONS:

Heat oven to 325°. Stud oranges with cloves. Place in baking pan with a little water, just enough to cover bottom of pan. Bake 30 minutes. Heat cider and cinnamon stick in large pan. Bring to boil and simmer covered 5 minutes. Add remaining ingredients and simmer uncovered 5 minutes longer.

Place in punch bowl and float baked oranges on top.

Spitznas Family
CORNISH SAFFRON BREAD

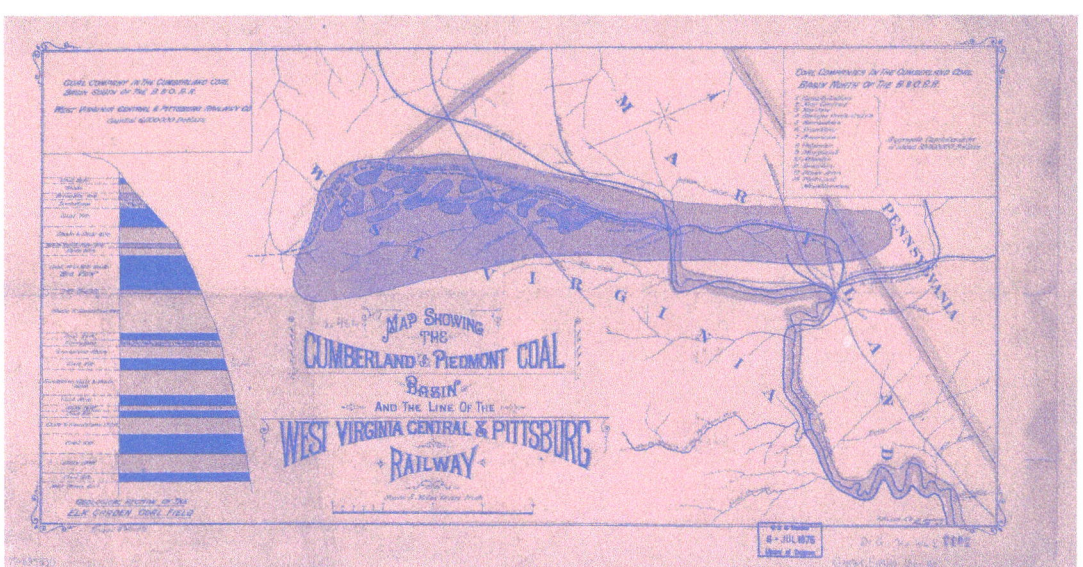

Among the "treasures" acquired in 1960 by the Maryland Department at the Enoch Pratt Free Library ("Maryland Room Acquires 'Treasures,'" Baltimore Sun, November 1960) is a copy of a cookbook put out in 1948 by the Maryland Home Economics Association. It is written in many different hands (with varying degrees of legibility).

Entitled "Maryland Cooking," the book contains 310 recipes. Three are for beaten biscuits, one for crab cakes. "Stuffed Country Ham" makes an appearance as well. The book is notable in that it draws from regions of Maryland where fewer community or historic cookbooks have been produced. Each of Maryland's counties had a committee gathering recipes for the book. Ethel Grove from Washington County contributed a recipe for "Maple Bavarian Cream."

Miners in Cumberland, MD

Maple syrup was once a prized product of Western Maryland. One recipe, for "Cornish Saffron Bread," is prefaced with a statement about how the bread was introduced to Frostburg by miners from Cornwall in the mid-1800s.

According to the Spitznas family of Frostburg, "in Cornwall, saffron bread is made on special occasions throughout the year, but in Western Maryland it became distinctly associated with Christmas."

In 1955, Dr. James E. Spitznas (1893-1958) and his wife Elizabeth (1911-1994) (who were then living in Baltimore County) shared the same recipe and story with Baltimore Sun food columnist Virginia Roeder. Roeder described Cornwall as the "land of King Arthur and his Knights of the Round Table," but Dr. Spitznas pointed out that the tradition of Cornish saffron bread "probably preceded King Arthur by many centuries," as the Phoenicians had been visiting Cornwall with packages of saffron for over 2,000 years. He recalled that the Frostburg post office would fill with fragrant packages of saffron each year when the Christmas holiday approached.

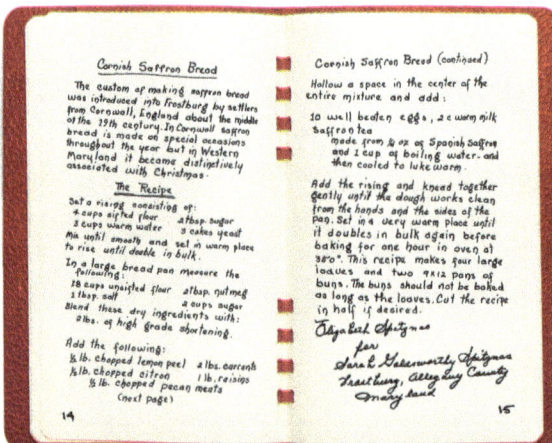

Cornish Saffron Bread is in a similar vein to Swedish "Lussekatter," saffron buns served around the holidays. Where Lussekatter are studded with a few raisins, the Cornish loaves are loaded with dried fruits and nuts throughout. The large quantities of ingredients in the Spitznas' recipe make enough bread for gift-giving.

Recipes from home economists occur throughout my Maryland cookbooks. Their influence is an under-appreciated aspect of culinary history. Perhaps if James E. Spitznas had not worked as a school superintendent, his family recipe would not have ended up in a book produced by home economics teachers, and I would never know about this uniquely Western Maryland tradition. —**KMH**

Cornish Saffron Loaf

Allegany County

Yields 2 loaves

Serving note: *clotted cream is traditional but a smear of some nice salted butter is a good alternative.*

  sweet dish

Cornish Saffron can be made as buns (rolls) or what Cornish people call a cake but I would say it is closer to a lightly sweet bread. This recipe is to make loaves which I find is a little easier to make but you can also section out the dough and roll them into rolls instead. The baking time would be about halved.

Unsurprisingly, saffron is a key ingredient in Cornish Saffron, it gives it both a floral flavor and the signature yellow hue. It is a spice more expensive than gold but can be found at Costco and online spice merchants in reasonable quantities for fairly affordable prices. You can even grow saffron crocuses here in Maryland and harvest your own! The yield is about 3 strands per bloom. —RR

INGREDIENTS:

- ¾ cups milk
- ½ teaspoon saffron threads, crumbled
- ½ cup warm water
- ½ tablespoon active dry yeast
- ¼ cup sugar
- ¼ teaspoon salt
- zest of 1 orange
- 4 cups bread flour
- ⅔ cup COLD unsalted butter, cubed
- 1 egg
- ¾ cup Zante currants (currants are traditional but I found lightly chopped dried tart cherries also worked very well)

DIRECTIONS:

Heat the **milk** and **saffron** in a tiny pot until bubbles begin to form around the edges of the pot. Remove from heat and allow to seep at least 20 minutes.

Meanwhile, stir together the **yeast**, a small sprinkle of **sugar** and warm (warm from the tap is fine) **water** in a small bowl and let that seep for 10-20 minutes.

In the bowl of a standmixer (or you can do all of this by hand if you'd prefer) whisk together the **sugar**, **salt**, **zest** and **flour**. Using the paddle attachment mix in the **butter** until it looks like slightly clumpy sand. Add both liquids and the **egg**. Mix until a soft dough forms.

Replace the paddle with the dough hook and knead until a smooth, elastic dough forms, about 5-10 minutes.

Place in a large, buttered bowl and cover with a tea towel. Allow to rise in a warm place for about an hour or until it's doubled in bulk.

Punch down the dough and work in the **currants** with your hands. Divide the dough in half and roll into two even spheres.

Let rest in the bowl, covered and side-by-side, for about 5 minutes while you butter 2 standard sized loaf pans.

Form the dough into rectangles and place in the pans. Cover both loaves with tea towels and return them to the warm place to rise again for about an hour or until the dough starts to creep above the rim of the pan.

Preheat oven to **350°**.

Brush each loaf with a small amount of milk if desired.

Bake for 40-50 minutes until golden brown.

Remove from pans and cool completely on wire racks.

Recipes from Little Bohemia
BARLEY CASSEROLE (Kuba)

Bohemian girl and boy in their backyard in Baltimore

In 1910, a parrot escaped from the home of Mrs. Caroline Bernard of 805 North Chester Street in East Baltimore. Officer Thomas P. Kirby was on the case. A known lover of animals, the policeman had previously recaptured stray goats, a canary, and a drunken monkey. Kirby's recovery of the parrot was the defining moment in the "big-hearted, rugged, fine-looking Irishman's" career. The bird, it was said, could talk in English, German, and Bohemian.

Although the trilingual parrot was remarkable, he wasn't even the only parrot in town who could speak Bohemian (now known as Czech). At one time, the neighborhood Kirby patrolled was called "Little Bohemia." The Czech population numbered somewhere around 10,000 when the Sun wrote about the officer's escapades in 1914.

Czech Christmas plate

In 1933, the newspaper printed listings of Christmas services - Catholic, Lutheran, Baptist. Under a section called "Other Churches," the Sun announced, "in St. Wencelaus' Church the old Bohemian Christmas carols will be sung; in the Polish churches, the old Polish carols; in the Italian churches, Italian carols." Such was life in Baltimore City.

The Sun wasn't always so flippant about Bohemian Christmas customs. In 1907 they ran an article describing "how these sturdy foreign-born folk celebrate Yuletide."

"Among Baltimore's adopted citizens, none is more strict in the observance of the feast than the Bohemian, who follows the customs of the old country to the letter." Festivities included Christmas trees, colorful candles, and rituals meant to induce good luck. Children hung stockings "in anticipation of the expected visit of the Ježíšek (Santa Claus)." Early morning mass at St. Wenceslaus Bohemian Catholic Church was a must.

There was also an elaborate meal which included "kuba," a dish made of dried mushrooms, pearl barley, and garlic and baked like a cake. Also essential to the meal was "the Bohemian turkey": a carp. "Bohemians would as soon do without their kuba and carp as Americans without their turkey, mince pie, and plum pudding," reported the Sun.

"Recipes from Little Bohemia," a cookbook produced by St. Wenceslaus, includes multiple recipes for carp dishes to be served on Christmas. Since carp is nearly impossible to purchase in the U.S., we adapted one of the book's two recipes for kuba.

The church looks much the same today as it did when its picture was printed on the cover of the book in 1984, although there are probably no Czech-speaking parrots around anymore. Standing at the edge of the ever-spreading Johns Hopkins medical campus, St. Wenceslaus remains a monument to a time when, as the Sun put it in 1907, "all Little Bohemia is anxiously and joyously waiting to sing out on Christmas Day 'Šťastné!' —a merry Christmas!" —**KMH**

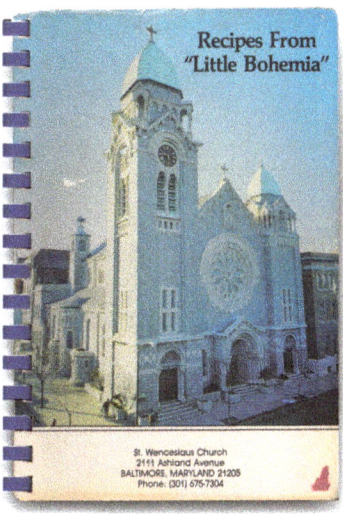

Czech parade in Baltimore, 1935

Houbový Kuba

 Baltimore City  **ŠŤASTNÉ!** Yields 8 servings main dish

This nutty, mushroom-packed dish has been popular in Czech households around Christmas time and on Christmas Eve for hundreds of years. Traditionally people would fast in the days leading up to Christmas, making hearty vegetarian dishes a popular choice. It's too cold to be mushroom picking in December so families would use mushrooms they dried during the warmer months. The tradition of using dried mushrooms has stuck but many families mix in fresh as well. I found that a mix of fresh and dried gave the dish the richest and most dynamic flavor. —RR

This recipe used hulled barley, often labeled simply as "barley", not pearl barley. If using pearl barley (also known as "pearled barley"), which has had the outer husk and bran layer removed, you may need to reduce the simmering time by about half.

INGREDIENTS:

- 1 lb hulled barley
- 1 cup sliced dried mixed mushrooms
- 4-6 cups of vegetable stock
- 2 onions, chopped
- 6 cloves garlic, minced
- 16 oz cremini mushrooms, sliced
- 1½ tablespoon caraway seeds
- 1½ tablespoon dried marjoram
- salt
- freshly ground black pepper

DIRECTIONS:

THE DAY BEFORE YOU WANT TO COOK:

In 2 medium bowls, soak the **barley** and **mushrooms** separately in warm water overnight.

THE NEXT DAY:

Drain the **mushrooms, reserving the liquid**. Chop the mushrooms (if desired) and set aside.

Drain and rinse the **barley**.

Heat a small amount of **butter** in a large skillet and add the **barley** and **rehydrated mushrooms**. Sauté until the barley looks golden. Add the **reserved mushroom water** and stir until it is absorbed. Add about 4 cups of stock and cook, stirring occasionally, until the barley is soft, about 40 minutes. Add more **stock** as needed—don't let the barley dry out.

Meanwhile, sauté the **onions** in a large skillet until nearly caramelized. Add the **seasonings**, **garlic**, and **fresh mushrooms** and sauté until the fresh mushrooms are fully cooked.

When the barley is nearly ready, preheat oven to **350°**. Add the onion mixture to the barley mixture and stir to evenly distribute all ingredients.

Lightly butter a 9x13 baking dish and pour the barley mixture into the dish.

Bake for 20 minutes or until lightly brown and crisped on top.

Note: recipe can be halved, if you do, bake in an 8x8 inch dish instead.

HOPPIN JOHN
for New Years

Quantico Muskrat Dinner

I. Henry Phillips

The 1958 "Historical Cookbook of the American Negro," by the National Council of Negro Women, opens with a photograph of Sojourner Truth and Abraham Lincoln, opposite recipes for the first of January: "Emancipation Proclamation Breakfast Cake" from Newark, New Jersey and "Western Beef Steak" from Denver. "The Emancipation Proclamation New Years' Day, 1863, is celebrated in all parts of the United States. The Council recipes… have been taken from the oldest files of Negro families," the book explains below the recipes.

The subsequent recipe is for "Southern Hopping John." No further explanations were needed for what this recipe meant and where it came from. The caption instead points out the similarity to another recipe in the book, for Haitian "Plate National," a dish of rice and beans enjoyed in Haiti, where Independence Day is January 1st. The book also includes a rice and beans recipe from Ghana. Together, the recipes imply a powerful message about food and heritage.

Oral histories given by local residents to the St. Mary's College Slackwater Center describe New Year's traditions in Southern Maryland throughout the 20th century to the present day.

Ent'd according to Act of Congress, A. D. 1863, by W. T. Carlton, in the Clerk's Office of the District Court of the District of Mass.

Residents of the Black farming communities there described New Year's as a kind of end to a season of celebration and relaxation. Philip H. Scriber, Sr. fondly recalled that "from Christmas to New Year no one did any work. They spent the whole holiday socializing. They made homemade cakes and root beer. In those days you didn't have the money, but you had the love."

Esther Smith described men in St. Mary's County trying to be the first to cross into others' households for good luck, "going to people's houses first thing in the morning on New Year's Day." Smith also described the custom of eating black-eyed peas and hogs' heads for New Year's. "Safeway stores and all... they have it ready for that day."

South Carolina-born Professor Jefferey Coleman explained that "collard greens meant, you know, money and prosperity and the black-eyed peas meant change."

I. Henry Phillips

In "Fighting Old Nep: The Foodways of Enslaved Afro-Marylanders 1634-1864," historian Michael Twitty wrote of his childhood memories of eating black-eyed peas on New Year's Day, as well as "putting them in everyone's wallet or pocketbook so that they would have money for the entire year." Twitty traced black-eyed peas' presence in Maryland to the 1750s.

Paul Henderson

"Collard greens meant money and prosperity and the black-eyed peas meant change."

Famed chef and Virginia native Edna Lewis described their use in her second book, "The Taste of Country Cooking": "They were not planted in the garden but were planted by farmers as a green manure crop. Before the sowing of wheat, when in full foliage, they were chopped into the soil. A week before, everyone was welcome to gather the green pods before the crop was chopped under" in the late summer and fall. Lewis mentioned the beans' African origin, noting that the legume was "always an exponent of agriculture" for its nitrogen and soil-building qualities.

Despite the long-standing presence of black-eyed peas in Maryland and Virginia, old Maryland recipes for Hoppin' John almost all come from South Carolina, where the dish probably originated.

A 1904 recipe in a boxed set of "Colonial Cook Cards" is attributed to the "Rose family" of Charleston. Reverend Hunter-Wyatt Brown, Jr., who was raised in Baltimore, contributed a recipe to the 1954 "Personal Recipes compiled by the Esther Circle St. Timothy's Church" of Catonsville cookbook. Wyatt-Brown was born in North Carolina but entitled his recipe "Hoppin' John (Old South Carolina)." The recipe that Rachel adapted was contributed by Greenville, South Carolina-born Louise Kelly to the 1975 community cookbook "300 Years of Black Cooking in St. Mary's County."

With West African-by-way-of-South Carolina origins, the deep-rooted tradition has been adopted by Marylanders of all races. No one wants to forego good luck on New Years' Day! —**KMH**

I. Henry Phillips

Hoppin' John

 St. Mary's County | Yields 12 servings | side dish

Serve it with collard greens (symbolizing money) and cornbread (symbolizing gold) to maximize your luck.

  ham **HOCKS**

There are so many versions and methods of what seems like a very basic dish of beans and rice. Traditionally in the South, it was made with another kind of cowpeas, field peas or Sea Island red peas, but they can be difficult to find outside of the Carolina low county and other parts of the South. As people who grew up with the dish moved north, they adapted to what was available locally. Most Maryland recipes call for black-eyed peas so that's what I used here.

The method is always up for debate as well. Many old recipes have you cook the rice in with the beans towards the end of the cooking time but I have not had the best of luck with that method—I end up with rice that is either too mushy or too dry and rarely just right. Some finish the rice off in the oven for this reason but I've figured out my preferred method is to split the difference a little.

I start out by cooking a huge ham hock in seasoned water, then I drain off some of the liquid and use it to either make the rice in a pan on the stove or better yet in the rice cooker. That way you get some nice flavor in the rice before you stir it all together.

This dish is served on New Year's Day because it contains two symbolic ingredients said to give you luck in the new year—black-eyed peas represent coins and pork is said to be lucky because pigs look forward when foraging, unlike chicken or turkeys which scratch backwards.—**RR**

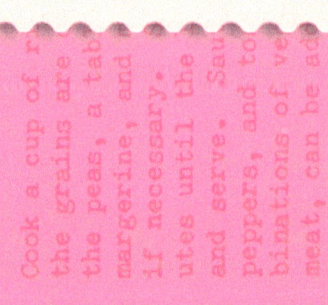

INGREDIENTS:

- **1** lb dried black-eyed peas

FOR THE HAM HOCKS:

- **1-2** lb ham hock
- **3** bay leaves
- **3** tablespoons black peppercorns
- **½** onion
- **10** cups chicken stock

FOR THE BEANS:

- **1** onion, diced
- **2** cloves garlic, sliced
- **2** stalks celery (with greens), diced
- **½** teaspoon cayenne
- **½-1** teaspoon dried thyme
- Freshly ground black pepper
- **2** tablespoons white vinegar
- **1** cup long grain rice

DIRECTIONS:

The night before you want to serve: soak the **beans** overnight in water. Drain when ready to cook.

FOR THE HAM HOCKS:

Place all **hock**, **bay leaves**, **peppercorns**, **onion** and **stock** in a large pot. Bring to boil for 5 minutes, reduce heat to simmer about 1 hour until the ham is tender.

Remove the pot from heat. Skim off any scum. Remove the ham hock and remove the meat from the bone into a bowl. Set aside the meat and discard the bone, onion and peppercorns.

Remove **2 cups liquid** to use to make the **rice**.

FOR THE RICE AND BEANS:

In a small pan, sauté the **onion**, **garlic** and **celery** until softened. Add to the remaining stock. Add the **beans** and **spices**. Add additional stock to cover the beans. Stir in the **vinegar**.

Meanwhile, cook the **rice** according to package instructions in your preferred method.

Cook the **beans** until tender, about 1 hour. During the last 15 minutes, stir in the **reserved meat** from the ham hock.

Stir in the rice and serve.

HOLIDAY TRADITIONS FROM THE OLD LINE STATE

I. Henry Phillips

Maryland
EGG NOG

"Christmas comes but once a year, when eggnog takes the place of beer."
– 1918

Egg nog recipe from Hendler's Creamery, Baltimore, MD 1950s

These days, Christmastime can feel tainted by materialism, compulsory spending, thoughtless gifts, and waste. Greedy corporations manipulate our nostalgia with limited edition Coke cans and the like. But there was a time, over a century ago, when things were simple and pure. Back in those days, before the Black Friday sales or department store extravaganzas, the Christmas holidays were more grounded, centered in the true reason for the season: getting #$@%-ed up.

Make no mistake – our agrarian ancestors indeed worked their fingers to the bone day in, day out for the most of the year. But when winter rolled around, the harvests were put up, and the hogs had been killed and cured, one of the primary duties to attend to was partying. Families would travel or host visitors. When possible, food was shared in all directions. Spirits were consumed, often to excess.

The large quantities called for in old eggnog recipes hearken to a time when a huge batch was made in late November to serve to guests throughout the season.

This annual cycle remained in the social DNA even as the nature of work changed, and more and more people flocked to cities and manned machines year round (or sat in offices and collected on the work of others). In this environment, things could get a little chaotic.

Especially in the rough-and-tumble environment of late 1800s Baltimore, the winter holidays correlated with a time of increased accidents, petty crimes, and some not-so-petty crimes.

In old newspapers, I found accounts of several incidents of murder or drugging by eggnog. The ubiquitous holiday beverage with its potent combination of liquors must have been a tempting vehicle for sinister motives in December.

More innocuously, eggnog was generally associated with the type of rowdiness that drew the finger-wagging of the temperance movement and the cautioning of elders. In 1890, two Baltimore men, aged 19 and 21, successfully used "egg-nogg" as a defense when they went to trial for stealing a horse and buggy on a lark.

Each year, news editorials appeared, admonishing would-be eggnog hellions to stop the insanity. In 1905, a Baptist reverend took to the pages of the Afro-American to decry the debauchery, firecrackers, and revealing clothing associated with Christmas revelry. Many young men, he warned, have their "lives blotted out" on this one day, and many young women "start to hell."

During the holiday season, temperance advocates gladly took on the title of "Anti Egg-Nog Movement" when holding meetings.

Still, the popularity of eggnog continued right on up to —and through— Prohibition. In 1921, the Sun declared that "eggnog is properly seasoned with real Jamaica rum, bootlegged at $8 a quart."

Although it was blamed for sowing mayhem, eggnog had its defenders. When in 1910 the Annapolis Capital paper quipped, "With eggs at 42 cents per dozen the Mint Julep Association is glad it does not belong to the Eggnog Clan," the Baltimore Sun indignantly reprinted the comment with a reply.
"Clan, sister? It is a hierarchy, a universal brotherhood, a winged saraband that measures its membership by the millions and counts its kingdoms by the stars." **—KMH**

> **"The enjoyments of the Christmas festival were accompanied, as usual, with the usual number of accidents, some resulting from the careless use of firearms, whilst others may perhaps be attributed to the too free use of egg-nogg and apple toddy."**
> – Baltimore Sun, 1868

Christmas in the South, Eggnog Party, 1870 drawn by W.L. Sheppard

HOTEL MEN BREATHE EASIER

Ban On Cocktails In West Caused An Awful Scare For A While Among Christmas Imbibers.

Law Will Not Stop Pleasure.

EGGNOG TO BLAME

HOSTS NEED NOT FEAR

TAKES EGGNOG AND ICY BATH

Benjamin Franklin, Of Ensor Street, Rescued From Harbor.

After imbibing too freely of eggnog yesterday evening, Benjamin Franklin, 1705 Ensor street, wandered aimlessly down to Pier 4 on Pratt street, and fell overboard. That he was not drowned was due to Capt. John Benton and W. P. Laugaker, of the schooner Anna Daniels which was lying at the pier.

Shortly after 7 o'clock Captain Benton heard cries of distress. He saw Franklin struggling in the water. With Laugaker in assistant, he threw the man a rope, and in a short time Franklin was pulled aboard the schooner.

ARREST OF A BOARDING HOUSE THIEF.—A few evenings since, John M. King, a boarder at the house of Mrs. Dunham, in Cincinnati, proposed to a room mate, named B. C. Randall, to treat the boarders of the house to egg-nogg, drugged with morphine, and while under its influence enter their bed chambers and rob them of their money. Randall assented to the arrangement with apparent good will, but after the departure of King, for a file and a pair of nippers, and the morphine, he revealed the matter to the boarders, who agreed to remain silent and allow the thing to go on, with the only difference in the arrangement that Randall should, by some means or other, substitute a paper of flour for that of morphine. The egg-nog was furnished, the deception practised, and at the usual hour all hands retired, but not to sleep, as they determined to watch King. The latter, about one o'clock, awoke Randall, and the two proceeded to ransack the house, until the boarders rallied, rushed in, and knocked King down. He soon confessed his guilt, and was held to answer. It is said he was engaged to be married to one of the young lady boarders.

Evelyn Clarkson Was Left Alone In Room With It, And—Well, Policeman Got Her.

In shame-faced manner Evelyn Clarkson, a rather good-looking woman of about 35 years of age who was arrested at Park avenue and Lexington street yesterday afternoon on a charge of being intoxicated, told Justice Eppler, that it was stolen egg-nog which proved her undoing.

She had visited a friend, the friend had given her two glasses of eggnog of Thanksgiving brew. Then the friend had left the room. The drink tempted her, so when she was alone with it—

Patrolman Dash, who arrested her, said she hadn't given him any trouble, so the magistrate told her to go and to avoid being isolated in company with the eggnog in the future.

KIDNAPPING MERELY AN EGGNOG INCIDENT

Unwilling Auto Passenger Victim Of Cheer, Not Abduction, Is Claim.

EGG NOG

I "created" this recipe by calculating average amounts of about thirty Maryland eggnog recipes, leaving out oddball additions like evaporated milk or cloves. Source recipes ranged from the 1800s through the modern-day. Very little about eggnog has changed over that time period, other than the flavor of peach brandy. If you don't like artificial flavors, make sure to get good brandy. —KMH

DIRECTIONS:

Beat eggs until smooth and yellow. Gradually beat in sugar, followed by liquors, vanilla (if using) and finish with milk and cream. Optional: top with beaten egg whites or fold them in last. **Top with nutmeg if desired.**

- 12 eggs (separated)
- 1 ¼ pint brandy (peach if you can find it, apple is the likely option)
- ½ pint Bourbon
- 1 tsp vanilla extract (optional)
- ½ pint Jamaican rum
- nutmeg (optional)
- 3 pints cream
- 2 pints milk
- 9 oz sugar (or to taste)

FESTIVE MARYLAND RECIPES

Elizabeth Ellicott Lea's
NEW YEARS CAKES

In 1906, The Frederick News printed a whimsical explanation for the "baker's dozen." A Dutch baker in the 1600s bickered with an "ugly woman" over whether a dozen was twelve or thirteen. "The shrillness of her voice did not mean anything to his slow Dutch mind," the story explained. "The hag left the shop" with only twelve "fresh New Year's cakes." The baker's shop became cursed until he conceded that a dozen was thirteen.

The "New Year's cakes" (cookies were often known as cakes or "little cakes" up through the late 19th century) mentioned in this fascinatingly spiteful fable were most likely meant to be a type of seed cake, said to originate with Dutch settlers in New York.

In 1884, the Oakland, Maryland Republican wrote of the "descendants of the old Hollanders" and their custom of making thin cookies with butter, eggs, sugar, and caraway seeds. (Hopefully, the inclusion of flour was implied.) The paper reported that people would go door-to-door with baskets on New Year's Day to collect the cookies.

THE BAKER'S DOZEN

How the Extra Tale of Numbers Arose in Trade.

Some persons, including a few encyclopaedists, are inclined to think that the baker's dozen originated when heavy fines were considered necessary to counterbalance light weights, and the bakers, in order to insure full weight, took the precaution to add an additional unit. Some have called it the devil's dozen, because thirteen was the number of witches who used to ride their broomsticks to the "Black Mass" of Satan. The baker's great book in the Astor Library has another story of its origin.

Jan Pietersen, of Amsterdam, was a good churchman, but nevertheless he was afraid of being bewitched. On the last night of 1654 he sat in his bakeshop trying to keep out the evil spirits by priming himself with a glass of good spirits. Sales had been brisk. There were no customers in the shop for the moment, and he sat back, meditating on the gains he would make on the morrow, when the fresh New Year's cakes were put on sale. He was startled by a sudden rap. An ugly woman pushed the door open.

"Give me a dozen New Year's cookies," she cried in a shrill voice.

The shrillness of her voice did not mean anything to his slow Dutch mind. It only annoyed him.

"Well, then, you needn't speak so loud," said Jan. "I'm not deaf."

"A dozen!" she screamed. "Give me a dozen. Here are only twelve."

"Well, then, twelve is a dozen."

"One more! I want a dozen."

"Well, then, if you want another go to the devil and get it."

The hag left the shop, but from that night Jan had trouble. The shop seemed to be bewitched. His cakes were stolen. Either his bread was so light that it soared up the chimney, or so heavy that the supports of the oven gave way beneath the burden. His wife became deaf; his children went wild. His trade took wings and settled in the shops of his rivals. Three times the old woman returned, and each time was directed to the devil's sanctum. At last, in despair, the baker called upon St. Nicholas to

Children making Christmas cookies

When Rachel looked into this recipe herself, she pointed out to me that there was no apparent connection to actual Dutch traditions or modern-day recipes. Confusion may have stemmed from the Pennsylvania Dutch, who are actually from Germany (aka "Deutschland"), and have a similar cookie known as "Apees."

Seed cakes made with caraway or other seeds had long been used to commemorate the harvest in Europe. Harvest customs may have drifted and morphed into Christmas celebrations, which in turn stretched into the "New Year."

"Dutch" New Year cakes were popular throughout the northeastern United States but were most commonly associated with New York. Although the cookies appeared in bestselling cookbook author Eliza Leslie's 1851 "Directions for Cookery" as "Apees", a nearly identical recipe appears later in the book as "New York Cakes," noting that they were similar to "New Year Cakes."

According to historian William Woys Weaver in "A Quaker Woman's Cookbook," **Leslie's recipe can be traced back to the cooking school of Elizabeth Goodfellow in Philadelphia. Cookie formulas are similar in general, but earlier versions of this cookie may appear as far back as the first American cookbook, 'American Cookery,' published by Amelia Simmons in 1796.**

Elizabeth Ellicott Lea

Eliza Leslie's many books were wildly popular and influential (and in fact, her own parents were from Cecil County), but Weaver draws a closer connection between Maryland-born Goodfellow, whose husband was a Quaker clockmaker, and Quaker cookbook author Elizabeth Ellicott Lea, herself a Marylander. "Lea's contact with Goodfellow may have been indirect, but it is clear that many of Lea's friends and acquaintances had attended the cooking school," resulting in many versions of Goodfellow's recipes making their way into Lea's 1845 book, "Domestic Cookery."

"For rural Quakers, [these cookies were] a special treat for Children at New Year's... related to New Year's cookies that were associated with the Dutch settlers in Colonial New York. Those cookies were often shaped with elaborate carved molds. The leavening in them was potash or pearl ash."

– William Woys Weaver, "A Quaker Woman's Cookbook."

I first noticed this recipe in a handwritten manuscript at the Maryland Center for History and Culture; a personal cookbook belonging to Becky Amos, wife of a Baltimore bricklayer. That recipe, it turned out, was copied verbatim from Lea's. That's how these things often worked. Another manuscript at MCHC, belonging to Margaret Howard, contained a different "New Year Cakes" recipe. That recipe was simply a list of ingredients: 8 lbs of flour, 2.5 lbs of sugar, 1.5 lbs of butter, and caraway seeds "if you like them."

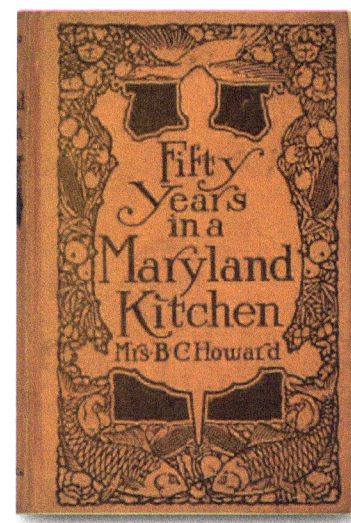

The cookies appeared again in 1873 when Mrs. B.C. Howard's cookbook "Fifty Years in a Maryland Kitchen" contained a recipe very similar to Lea's, with more butter and a pinch of salt, swapping out the saleratus with its more modern equivalent, baking soda. Lea flavored her New Year's Cakes with nutmeg or lemon, while Howard used caraway, but the recipes have similar wording and quantities. It certainly wouldn't be the only recipe adapted from Lea's book into Howard's. Both women belonged to wealthy Maryland families, but Lea lived a more agrarian lifestyle in Montgomery County, while Howard lived on the "Belvidere" estate in Baltimore City, attended by enslaved people and later, servants.

Belvidere estate of Mrs. B.C. Howard

This recipe wending its way from its murky "Dutch" origins, to a Philadelphia Cooking school, to a Quaker family of known abolitionists, to the formerly-slaveholding upper crust of 19th-century Baltimore is an example of the social webs that shaped Maryland cuisine. It's uncertain whether these cookies were commonly shared on New Year's in this state, but the recipe lived its own life within the pages of these cookbooks. —**KMH**

New Year's Cookies

For this recipe, I modernized the very old original recipe to be a little less labor intensive—slicing the cookies instead of rolling them out—and flavorful by adding some additional spices to the suggested nutmeg. The cookies are thought to be an evolution from seed cakes, a muffin-like baked good that unsurprisingly was full of seeds but I found a lot of conflicting histories about the cookies. Most New Year's Cookie recipes appeared to be from the same source which provided virtually no context and I went down the rabbit hole. It's a culinary mystery I didn't feel I was able to fully solve.

As a nod to their apparent seed cake beginnings, I used confectioners' sugar in the cookies for a more cake-like texture and left them slightly thick. The second reason I turned this recipe into a slice and bake icebox cookie was while I couldn't find any mention of consuming caraway for luck on New Year's Day, people often eat round foods to symbolize the last year coming full circle and fresh start beginning or to represent coins and hopes for wealth in the new year. —RR

Montgomery County

Yields 6 dozen

sweet dish

wealth in the **NEW YEAR**

INGREDIENTS:

- 1 cup butter, at room temperature
- 1 cup confectioners sugar
- 3 eggs, at room temperature
- 1 tablespoon vanilla
- 3 cups flour
- 1 tablespoon caraway seeds
- ½ teaspoon nutmeg
- ½ teaspoon cinnamon
- ½ easpoon allspice
- ½ teaspoon salt

DIRECTIONS:

In the bowl of a stand mixer, beat together the **butter** and **sugar** until light and fluffy.

Beat in the **eggs** and **vanilla**.

Add the **flour** and **spices**. Mix until a thick dough forms.

Lay out two 9x13 inch sheets of parchment.

Divide the dough in half.

Use your hands to shape each half into 2-inch-thick logs about 12 inches long.

Roll each one in one sheet of parchment paper so it looks like a giant saltwater taffy.

Refrigerate the dough for one hour or until it is very cold and solid feeling.

Preheat oven to **350°**. Line 4 baking sheets with parchment paper. Set aside.

Unroll the dough. Slice the dough into ¼ inch slices.

Place the cookies on the prepared baking sheets about ½ inch apart.

Bake 12-14 minutes or until the bottoms are golden brown.

Remove to wire rack and cool completely.

Store leftovers in airtight containers at room temperature.

Ladies of the Bethel
CHOP-CHAE

After the Immigration and Nationality Act of 1965 removed discriminatory barriers to moving to the United States, Maryland gained a new population of Korean-born citizens. Naturally, these newly-minted Marylanders brought their celebrations with them. In the 60s and 70s, newspapers began to report on the festivities. A 1970 Lunar New Year event held at the Korean embassy in Washington, D.C. attracted Korean-born Marylanders from around the state. Helen Giblo, a reporter from the Annapolis Capital, described for readers the galbi and "kimchie, a dish that is a way of life in the Land of Morning Calm." Also served was "dduk guk," Rice Cake Soup - a Korean New Year essential.

A group of people eating a meal in Korea c. 1900

The Bethel Korean Presbyterian Church of Baltimore was founded in June of 1979, with a parish made up of seven families. "Everyone was on the same boat, sometimes literally," Pastor Billy Park told the Baltimore Sun in 2002. By then, more than 1,700 people were attending Sunday services at the church.

The "Ladies of the Bethel" did not include a recipe for Rice Cake Soup in their 1986 eponymous cookbook. Perhaps the authors felt that the rice cakes were too difficult to acquire or to make. The recipes in the book often reflect the constraints of limited access to ingredients, and provide a contrast to today's vicinity around the church (which moved to Ellicott City in 1987), an area now strewn with multiple international grocers such as H-Mart.

The book does contain many other traditional recipes, with the intention, as Susan Y. Park, the cookbook chairperson wrote, "to introduce as many Korean recipes as possible to those who are accustomed to Western food."

Japchae is one of the most popular Korean dishes for holidays. The recipe in "Ladies of the Bethel" (spelled in the book as "Chop-Chae") is clearly written by someone with a love of the dish, and its instructions read almost like a monologue.

"After you fry onion and scallion, do the beef so that the spicy flavor can soak into the meat from the pan. Store cooked ingredients in a large bowl so that you can mix them with the noodle all together. Cut up the noodle crisscross a couple of times with scissors to the desired length. Mix all ingredients in the bowl together and add the seasoning to your liking. Sesame seeds or sesame oil should be added at the end to enhance the flavor. Serve when warm."

Note the serving suggestions at the end. Although we may never know her name, the recipe's anonymous author commands our attention. As evidenced by an errata sheet at the front of the book with such corrections as "dash of cinnamon" to "½ teaspoon" and "1 tsp salt" to "1½ tsp salt," it was important to the "Ladies of the Bethel" that cookbook users experience the recipes at their very best. —**KMH**

Korean Christmas cards in the Enoch Pratt Free Library collection

Japchae
(잡채)

Howard County

main dish

Yields 6 servings

This is another dish that is made for celebrations that has a lot of variations. I find that a double dose of mushrooms, both fresh and rehydrated dried, gives the dish an additional depth of flavor and texture interest, but that may be too many mushrooms for some!

I was taught to soak my noodles instead of boiling them so that's what I did here, but you can follow the package instructions of your noodles. Even if you boil your noodles, you still must soak your dried mushrooms, so keep that in mind when figuring out the timing.

The ingredient list looks long but it's largely the same ingredients repeated as to season each step and layer of the dish. It all comes together relatively quickly. —RR

INGREDIENTS:

FOR THE NOODLES AND MUSHROOMS:

- 5 dried shiitake mushrooms (can substitute 1-2 wood ear mushrooms instead)
- 16 oz dangmyun (Korean sweet potato noodles)
- 3 teaspoons soy sauce (I use Sempio brand jin-ganjang 진간장)
- 1 teaspoon sesame oil
- ½ teaspoon rice wine or mirin
- ½ teaspoon sugar

FOR THE BEEF:

- ½ lb flank steak, cut, against the grain into 3" long thin strips
- 1½ tablespoons soy sauce
- 1 tablespoon sugar
- 1 tablespoon sesame oil
- ½ tablespoon rice wine or mirin
- 1 clove garlic, minced

FOR THE VEGETABLES:

- ½ medium onion, thinly sliced into halfmoons
- ½ large carrot, cut into matchsticks
- 4 fresh shiitake mushrooms, thinly sliced
- 1 bunch scallions, greens cut into 2-inch long pieces and white ends minced
- 8 oz baby spinach

FOR THE SAUCE:

- 3 tablespoons soy sauce
- 1 tablespoon sugar
- 1 tablespoon rice wine or mirin
- 1 tablespoon sesame oil
- 1 tablespoon sesame seeds

DIRECTIONS:

About 2 hours before you want to start to cook—soak the **dried mushrooms** and the **noodles** in a large bowl of warm water for at least two hours, they should roughly double in size. I like to place the mushrooms in a sieve in the same bowl of water as the noodles. Drain the noodles, return them to the bowl and set aside. Place the mushrooms to a small bowl and marinate them in the **remaining ingredients** until you need them.

Combine **all ingredients for the beef** in a small bowl. Set aside.

Whisk together the **sauce ingredients** in another small bowl. Sprinkle 3/4 of the sauce over the noodles and mix until the noodles absorb the sauce.

In a large skillet, sauté the **carrot**, **fresh mushrooms** and **onions** until soft in a small amount of oil. Add to the noodles and toss to evenly distribute the ingredients.

Blanch the **spinach** and toss it in the noodle bowl.

Add the marinated beef and marinated, rehydrated mushrooms to the same pan the vegetables were in. Add a drizzle of oil if needed. Sauté for 2-5 minutes or until beef is cooked through.

Add the meat mixture to the noodle bowl and toss to evenly distribute all ingredients. Sprinkle with the remaining sauce and toss again.

Serve at room temperature.

HOLIDAY TRADITIONS FROM THE OLD LINE STATE

KINKLINGS
a.k.a. Fastnachts

Shrove Tuesday (1882) Gunnar Berndtson

"Maryland Germans whose ancestors, like the Pennsylvania Dutch, came from the Palatinate, need no reminder that Tuesday is Fastnacht Day. By this time, they either have stocked the pantry shelf with the necessary ingredients for home-made fastnachts or they have placed an order with one of the bakeries that still make the real things." – The Baltimore Sun, 1958

A cookbook manuscript in the Symington-Slingluff papers at the Maryland Center for History and Culture contains a recipe for "Quick Kinklins": fried dough made with lard, sugar, egg, flour, and baking powder. The book belonged to Mary Imogen Dorsey.

Dorsey was born near Frederick in 1874. She compiled her recipe book around 1886, pasting recipes over the pages of an old ledger. The "Quick Kinklins" recipe is attributed to "Gitlinger" - probably a Frederick-area friend or neighbor. Although most "kinkling" recipes would not have used baking powder, the fact that this one did was probably what made it notable enough to write down. The leavening shortcut took America by storm in the late 1800s. As a result, "Quick Kinklins" is the only recipe in the Old Line Plate database with anything resembling "kinkling" in the name.

Another book at MCHC, from the John Gilman D'Arcy Paul collection, contains a recipe entitled "Vos Nachts An Easter Cake German." This recipe, for yeast-risen dough flavored with cinnamon, nutmeg, and rose water, dates to about 1880. The dough is rolled thin and cut "in squares or diagonally or any way you choose," risen again, fried in lard, then dusted with sugar. The recipe is attributed to "Grand Ma." Sadly, the author of the book is unknown.

"'Eat a doughnut on Shrove Tuesday,' say the Pennsylvania Dutch, 'and live a year longer.'.."

When I was a child, my mother and aunts all fondly recalled an annual feast of doughnuts that I thought were called "fox knocks." Like "Vos Nachts," this was a mishearing of fastnacht, a German word for the festivities leading up to Lent.

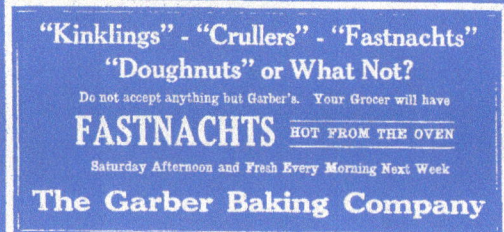

The doughnuts are the German version of the various pre-Lenten pastries like King Cakes and the Polish Pączki. Like scrapple, which is derived from the German dish panhas, the fastnacht tradition made its way to Maryland and took on a life of its own.

In the Frederick area, fastnachts often go by the unique name "Kinklings" and are celebrated with an annual flutter of news mentions and a rush on bakeries for "Kinkling Day" - a.k.a. Fat Tuesday.

As an adult, I finally got together with my aunt and cousin to make the legendary "fox knocks". It turned out that fastnachts were not a deep-running tradition in my family. The recipe we used came to us via 1960s columnist Clementine Paddleford, whose syndicated column disseminated many recipes and their stories far and wide. She used the doughnuts' full German name "Fastnachts Küchlie." "Küchlie" roughly translates to 'cakes,' and if you stretch your imagination, you might just hear that word as "kinkling."

Paddleford's article was entitled "Doughnuts Everybody Remembers," which is very appropriate, even if everybody doesn't remember how to say "Fastnachts." —KMH

"Today is Kinkling Day and the smell of hot grease and fresh kinklings permeates many homes. Some people say that for good luck some of the kinklings must be fed to the chickens. This is done in a lot of cases, but in most instances the housewife would rather do the eating.

Others declare that today is pancake day, and that tomorrow is kinkling day. Those interested can settle it among themselves."

– The Frederick News, Tuesday March 7, 1916

HOLIDAY TRADITIONS FROM THE OLD LINE STATE

Kinklings

 Frederick County  sweet dish

Best served same day they are made.

  Yields about 2-½ dozen doughnuts

Many recipes for these doughnuts make an absolutely massive amount. Dozens and dozens of doughnuts. Not only is that a ton of work and you would need some very large bowls to let all that dough rise, but these doughnuts are best fresh from the fryer. This is not a make ahead snack.

I did some tinkering and came up with a recipe that makes enough doughnuts to share with your friends, maybe not the entire neighborhood but some friends, that also is as streamlined and accessible as possible. It's well worth the effort and I promise people will be very impressed that you made potato doughnuts at home. They are so light and fluffy it will be hard to eat any other kind of doughnut ever again! —RR

QUICK TIP

Doughnut making goes very quickly! Be ready with paper towel lined platters to drain and bowls/plates of sugar ready to dip your doughnuts in before you start frying.

INGREDIENTS:

- 1 Russet potato (about 1/2 pound), peeled and diced
- ¾ cup sugar
- 1 tablespoon active dry yeast
- 1 egg, at room temperature
- ⅓ cup butter
- 3 cups flour
- oil, for frying
- more granulated sugar for coating the doughnuts

This was my method for frying the doughnuts by myself:
I put two doughnuts in the hot oil, when they were ready to flip, flipped them and I added two more. When the first two were ready I removed them to the platter and flipped the "new" batch. I added two new doughnuts to the pan to replace the ones I removed. Then I used tongs to dip the hot doughnuts from the platter in the sugar and returned them to the platter. By the time they were sugared, the next set of two was ready and I started over. I made all the doughnuts in about 20 minutes. I found it easier to work alone (my kitchen is tiny!) but you may find it better to work with someone who can be sugaring the doughnuts while you are frying.

DIRECTIONS:

In a small pot, boil the **potatoes** in at least 2 cups of water. Remove and **reserve** 3/4 cup of the potato cooking water. Drain and mash the potatoes until smooth.

In a medium bowl, stir together the mashed **potatoes**, reserved **potato cooking water**, and **sugar**. Allow to cool a few minutes until it is closer to room temperature and whisk in the **yeast**. Cover with a tea towel and let the mixture rest for 15-20 minutes. It should look foamy and like the yeast is starting to do something. If it doesn't, start over.

Meanwhile, melt the **butter** in a small saucepan and set aside to allow to cool slightly.

Whisk the potato mixture into a large bowl or bowl of a stand mixer through a metal sieve.

Stir in the **egg**. Stir 1 cup of the flour until the egg looks mixed in, about a minute. Add the second cup and mix until dough starts to form around the dough hook (or in your bowl around your spoon if mixing by hand), about 3-5 minutes. Stream in the melted butter as the mixer goes (or mix it in by hand a little at a time). Mix 1 minute then slowly add the remaining 1 cup of flour in as the mixer is going with the dough hook (or use a spoon and some muscle) until the dough forms a large ball and has completely come away from the sides of the bowl. Remove to a larger, buttered bowl that has room for the dough to double in size. Cover with a tea towel and put in a warm place to rise for 3 hours.

On a clean, floured surface, roll out the dough into an 1/2-inch-thick rectangle. Cut into large 3x3" squares. Place each on a large baking sheet or platter at least an inch apart. Make a little dimple with your finger tip in the middle of each doughnut but don't push all the way through. Cover with a tea towel and allow to rise again in a warm place for 30-45 minutes.

Heat a few inches of oil in a large walled skillet or Dutch oven to **365**°. Meanwhile, line some platters or cookie sheets with paper towels. Pour some more granulated sugar in a shallow bowl or plate.

Working in batches, fry the doughnuts until golden brown on both sides, flipping once, about 2 minutes per side. Drain briefly on paper towel lined plates. (see note for details about how I did this myself)

Dip both sides of each doughnut in granulated sugar and serve.

Best served the same day they are made.

HOLIDAY TRADITIONS FROM THE OLD LINE STATE

Mildred Hailey's
GINGER CREAM CAKE

"In speaking of our adopted citizens of foreign birth, we hardly ever make any mention of the Welsh miners who have settled in Allegany and Garrett Counties, although they form a most industrious and intelligent portion of the mining population. We have no information as to their numbers, but from the fact that they have at least two churches at Frostburg, we infer that there must be not less than five hundred Welsh families living near the coal fields." - the Baltimore American, 1873

The previous owner of my copy of the circa 1980 "Favorite Recipes from the Women's Welsh Club of Baltimore" tried at least two of its recipes. In the margins next to the recipe for "Welsh Bara Brith (Speckled Bread)" they wrote "1981 good St. David's Day." Beside the recipe for "Welsh Ginger Cream Cake (Teisen Hufen Sinsir)" they wrote "St. David's Day 1981 odd but good."

The feast of Saint David, patron saint of Wales, is observed on March 1st, the anniversary of his death in 589 AD. The holiday is a celebration of all things Welsh, from food to clothing to flora.

Although no single wave of immigration resulted in a large Welsh community in Baltimore, people of Welsh origin came to work in the city's industries, or ended up there via migration from Appalachia, the Peach Bottom Slate Region, and the "Welsh Tract" of Pennsylvania.

In the 1830s, miners were recruited from Wales to Western Maryland due to their familiarity with the equipment and technology used by the George's Creek Coal and Iron Company.

The superintendents of the company kept journals, which chronicle the predictable conflicts between management and workers, as well as scuffles between Welsh and Cornish miners. In 1839, one journal mentioned St. David's Day as a "holiday among the Welsh" employees.

The Frostburg Mining Journal newspaper announced St. David's Day celebrations at the Mt. Zion Welsh Baptist Church annually starting in 1902.

Welsh miners had immigrated since 1845 to work in the Peach Bottom Slate Region, which spans from Pennsylvania into Harford County, where there is a town named Cardiff, after the Capital of Wales.

In Baltimore, Welsh workers moved into a section of the Canton neighborhood that was briefly known as "the Welsh Colony." In 1928, a Baltimore Sun writer described the area, which by then had only remnants of its past, including a church on Toone Street and a row of dilapidated houses on Clinton.

The Welsh residents of Baltimore may have dispersed throughout the metro area, but they still held onto their culture. In the 1970s, The Women's Welsh Club of Baltimore held meetings at the Enoch Pratt Free Library. "All women of Welsh origin or wives of men of Welsh origin are invited," read newspaper announcements.

Some of the notices stated that Mildred Hailey, a club member "who was born in Wales," would be a guest speaker.

Hailey, maiden name Mildred Jones, was born and raised in Cardiff. She came to the United States after marrying William Thomas Hailey, an American serviceman she met while she was working for the Red Cross.

Her 2012 Baltimore Sun obituary mentions many places the Haileys lived, but singled out Linthicum Heights because during her time there, Mildred "provided 'delicious food for many festivities,'" including her Welsh cakes based on an old family recipe."

Is St. David's Day one of Maryland's sacred holidays? Well, maybe not anymore. But Mildred's "odd but good" cake represents the best of celebrations anywhere – communities small and large finding a reason to feast, share, and remember. It could be a chance to start a new tradition, or at least to try something new, leaving a memory to be preserved in the margins of a cookbook. —**KMH**

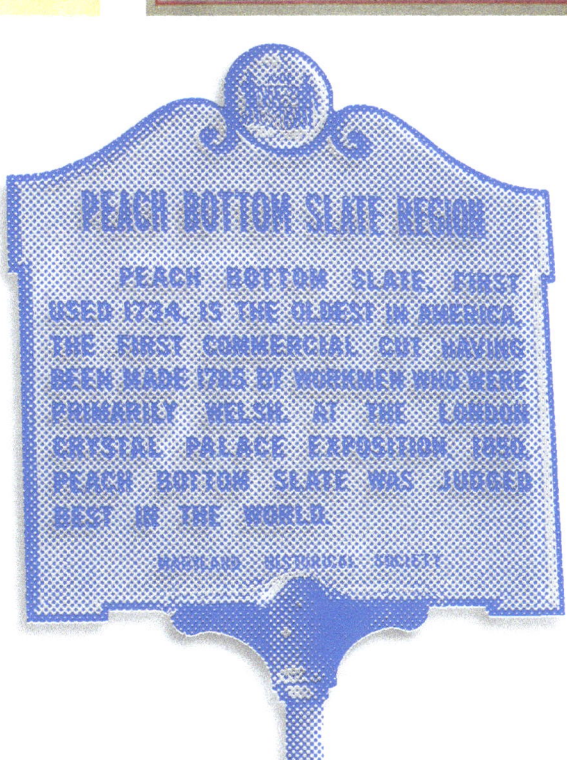

Welsh Ginger Cream Cake
(Teisen Hufen Sinsir)

 Anne Arundel County  whipped cream on the side — Yields 8 servings — sweet dish

This was an interesting recipe to work with. I could not find a traditional Welsh recipe that was similar to this cake. I did find a lot of gingerbread and loaf shaped tea cakes. The names translate directly to ginger cream cake but as I found, in Wales it wasn't uncommon for a recipe to be called ginger cake or gingerbread and not actually contain ginger! I found cream cakes that did not have cream but were to be served with a cream tea—which is an afternoon ritual of tea, scones (or other baked goods), clotted cream and jam.

In reading the recipe I was pretty sure it was tweaked in some way already—it called for molasses instead of dark treacle (a mixture of cane molasses and syrup) which is more common in Welsh recipes and it's an uniced cake served with lemony whipped cream in the middle. I was not surprised by the note next to the recipe that said it was "odd". It would have been slightly odd by 1981 to serve an uniced cake. Uniced cakes with only buttercream or whipped cream fillings are more common during times of rationing or economic hardship because it uses fewer expensive and often limited ingredients like butter or cream. By the 1980s fluffy frosted cakes had been standard for decades.

Of course, that's all guesswork on my part! It is also possible that the contributor simply didn't care for icing or turned a single layer cake served with whipped cream into a cake that would serve more and transport more easily.

I find whipped cream filled or topped cakes a little stressful. Once assembled, the race is on to finish the cake before it deflates and becomes soggy. Leftovers are not great. Keeping that in mind, I reimagined the cake a bit as a tea cake with plenty of whipped cream on the side. You can store the leftover cream in the fridge and the cake on the counter for about 3 days. Sliced cake will dry out faster so you may want to slice as you serve. —RR

WELSH GINGER CREAM CAKE
(TEISEN HUFEN SINSIR) — Mildred Hailey

2 1/2 c. flour
1/3 c. sugar
1 c. dark molasses
3/4 c. hot water
1/2 c. shortening
1 egg
1 tsp. baking soda
1 tsp. ground ginger
1 tsp. cinnamon
3/4 tsp. salt
whipped cream filling
powdered sugar

Heat oven to 325 degrees. Measure all ingredients except Whipped Cream Filling and powdered sugar into a bowl. Blend 1/2 minute on low speed, scraping bowl constantly. Beat 3 minutes at medium speed, scraping bowl occasionally. Pour into 2 greased and floured round layer pans 8"x1 1/2". Bake about 30 to 35 minutes, until a wooden pick inserted in center comes out clean. Cool. Fill layers with whipped cream filling. Sift powdered sugar over top of cake.

Whipped Cream Filling:

1 c. chilled whipping cream
1 Tbsp. lemon juice
1/4 c. powdered sugar
2 tsp. grated lemon peel

Beat whipping cream, sugar and lemon juice in chilled bowl until stiff. Fold in grated lemon peel.

INGREDIENTS:

FOR THE CAKE:

- ¼ cup sugar
- ¾ cup unsulfured black strap molasses
- ½ cup warm water
- ⅓ cup unsalted butter, at room temperature
- 1 teaspoon lemon zest
- 2 cups flour
- 1 teaspoon ground ginger
- ½ teaspoon ground cinnamon
- 1 teaspoon baking powder
- ½ teaspoon baking soda

FOR THE CREAM TOPPING:

- 1 cup cold heavy cream
- 1 tablespoon fresh lemon juice
- ½ cup confectioners' sugar
- 2 teaspoons lemon zest

DIRECTIONS:

For the cake:

Preheat oven to **350°**. Butter and flour a loaf pan.

In a large bowl or bowl of a stand mixer, beat together the **sugar**, **molasses**, **water**, **butter**, **egg** and **zest** until smooth. Add in the dry ingredients and beat until a smooth batter forms.

Scrape into the prepared pan and bake for 30-40 minutes or until a toothpick inserted into the center comes out clean. Cool in pan on wire rack for 3 minutes then invert on to the rack to cool completely.

Slice and serve with a bowl of **lemon whipped cream** to taste.

Store leftovers in an air tight container up to 3 days.

For the cream topping:

Beat whipping cream, sugar and lemon juice in chilled bowl until stiff. Fold in zest.

Serve immediately with the cake or refrigerate until ready to use.

HOLIDAY TRADITIONS FROM THE OLD LINE STATE

Jeanette Oettinger's
CHOCOLATE MACAROONS

One of the first Jewish-American cookbooks, Esther Levy's "Jewish Cookery Book," was published in 1871 in Philadelphia. Like many of its contemporaries, it included household tips for cleaning, repelling vermin, and treating common ailments like asthma, boils, and bad breath. There are many recipes for fish dishes: fried, broiled, potted, in salad. Soup recipes include ox-tail, gumbo, and matzo for Passover. Towards the back of the book, there was a Jewish calendar that listed holidays and dates for the Sabbath.

The preface warned against the idea that "a repast, to be sumptuous, must unavoidably admit of forbidden food." For Levy, cooking well was a matter of piety.

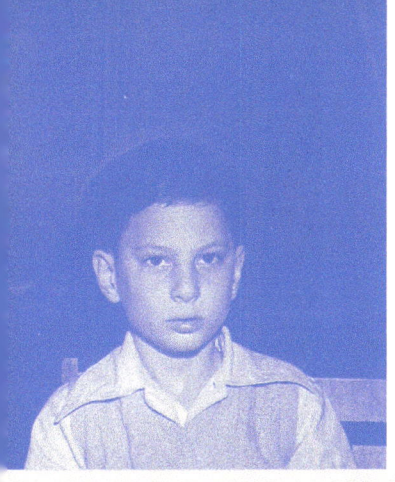

Rabbi Adolf Coblenz with three children during a Passover seder, 1947

HEBREW ORPHAN ASYLUM, BALTIMORE.

The authors of "Pots, Pans and Pie Plates & How to Use Them," one of the oldest Jewish cookbooks from this state, had a different approach. The book featured lots of regional favorites, including non-kosher fare like Maryland Fried Chicken (with cream gravy), five recipes for crab, and five for oysters. This was Chesapeake country after all.

The 1905 book may have broken from kosher tradition in order to appeal to a broader audience. It's more likely that the recipes simply reflected what the women who compiled the book liked to eat, and that they shared recipes accordingly.

Since 1895, the Hebrew Kindergarten and Day Nursery (for which "Pots, Pans and Pie Plates" was a fundraiser) had provided education to children, especially those of the influx of Russian Jewish immigrants to Baltimore.

A 1900 Baltimore Sun article about the school was headlined "Tots Play at Farming." In addition to the things "taught in all kindergartens," the Hebrew Day Nursery was teaching the children about farming and gardening, housekeeping and cooking. That year, the Sun also described how the kids would observe the Feast of Purim by reciting the story of Queen Esther and enjoying cake and ice cream.

"Pots, Pans and Pie Plates," not only raised funds through cookbook sales, but also through the ads found in the book, for everything from umbrellas, shoes, and upholstery, to sarsaparilla and corned beef.

After the many breads, pickles, pies, cakes, and puddings in the book, there is a section of "Passover Receipts." Mrs. Louis Levin contributed all five recipes, and all involve matzo meal.

Local newspapers occasionally reported on Passover, with a special curiosity for matzo. In March 1893, the Frederick News Post wrote that "a great many large bake shops in Baltimore have been engaged since the first of the year in turning out nothing but unleavened bread… A matzath [sic] cake is round, about four inches in diameter, slightly browned and having tiny air hole protuberances on its surface. They have a rather pleasant taste not unlike that of crackers, and make an excellent substitute for bread…"

Mrs. Jeanette Oettinger

Another popular Passover treat is macaroons, which contain no flour or leavening. "Pots, Pans and Pie Plates" contained several recipes for them. Mrs. Jeanette Oettinger (1841-1947) provided the one adapted here, containing chocolate and cloves. Oettinger and her husband Frank (1825-1911) immigrated from Germany, and became prominent philanthropists in Baltimore, involved with a network of charities aiming to uplift and acclimate impoverished and/or recently immigrated Jews at the turn of the 20th century. The umbrella organization, The Federated Jewish Charities, became part of "The Associated: Jewish Federation of Baltimore," which is still active today.

"Pots, Pans and Pie Plates" served its religious ends not through strict adherence to traditional dietary laws, but through its charitable cause. According to the Talmud, charity, or tzedakah, "is equal to all the other commandments combined." —**KMH**

Spiced Chocolate "Macaroons"

Baltimore City

Yields 3 dozen

sweet dish

These macaroons are more like what many people would think of as meringues—light, fluffy but crunchy on the outside—with the addition of melted chocolate than the coconut haystacks you might see at supermarkets in springtime. Desserts made with egg whites as a key ingredient or leavening agent are popular during Passover when use of fermented grains is prohibited.

Today coconut macaroons are the signature American Ashkenazi Passover treat while macaroons made with almonds (not to be confused with the French macaron which is a sandwich cookie made with ground almonds) or other nuts are more commonly found in Sephardic and Mizrahi communities. At the time this cookbook was published, coconut and most nuts would have been a relatively rare and expensive treat, so it makes sense to provide an accessible macaroon that quite likely predated the coconut version and would satisfy everyone. —**RR**

INGREDIENTS:

- 6 egg whites (save the egg yolks for another recipe)
- 2 oz unsweetened baking chocolate
- 2½ cups confectioners' sugar
- ½ teaspoon cinnamon
- ¼ teaspoon ground cloves

DIRECTIONS:

Preheat oven to **220°**. Line 2 cookie sheets with parchment.

In the bowl of stand mixer (you can use a hand mixer or a whisk but it takes a long time and you will need help in a future step) whip the **egg whites** until a stiff peak forms. This is when the egg whites are smooth, shiny, and the "peak" that remains when you remove the whisk can stand straight up without folding back on itself.

Meanwhile, in a large bowl, grate the **chocolate** (I used the same grater I would use to zest a lemon) into the **confectioners' sugar**. Whisk in the **spices** until evenly distributed.

Once stiff peaks have formed, keep the mixer going (here is where you will need a friend if you don't have a stand mixer) and spoon the sugar mixture into the egg whites, making sure it is fully incorporated between each addition.

When you are out of sugar, stop mixing and quickly begin to place approximately 2 tablespoon sized dollops on the lined baking sheets. Repeat until all the mixture is gone.

Bake for 1 hour or until the dollops look dry and "set" and not like shiny raw egg.

Turn off the oven and allow them to completely cool in the oven, about 1 hour.

EASTER PIES
from Little Italy

Ida Cippolini Esposito gave an oral history to the University of Baltimore in 1979. In it, she described Easter in Baltimore's Little Italy. She told the Langsdale Library's Neighborhood Heritage Project, "it seemed like you just stopped, everything stopped in the house."

"By Holy Thursday your house would be immaculate, everything had to be clean, and you'd go out visiting all the churches." She said that her family would spend days touring local churches, including those of other Catholic immigrant groups like the nearby Polish churches, Holy Rosary and Saint Stanislaus.

The one thing that didn't stop for Easter festivities was food. "That's all the women did," she said.

The Neighborhood Heritage Project collected oral history interviews from different Baltimore neighborhoods. Nearly 30 of them are from Little Italy. Within these are stories of immigration, family, poverty, religion, and life in an ever-changing community.

The narratives in the archive depict an era when Little Italy was called a "slum;" experiences adjusting to life in a new city and country; and the intersecting lives of Baltimore's Italian, Jewish, and Black residents.

The food stories are varied. Some people recalled receiving donated canned goods, while others owned grocery stores. Wine was fermented in basements.

Esposito's grandparents made their own **salami,** **"galbobloos,"** and **"brazoot."**

Little Italy, Baltimore

Home shrine in East Baltimore

A closer look at the food of Little Italy is offered in cookbooks like "Italian American Favorite Recipes," compiled in 1982 by the American Committee on Italian Migration (A.C.I.M), and "Let's Cook Italian," a decade later by the Little Italy Lodge. These are newer cookbooks by my collection's standards, but recipe contributors often shared beloved traditional foods. Josie Platerote Giorgilli (1927-2010) shared a recipe in "Let's Cook Italian" for an Easter Pie filled with meats and hard-boiled eggs. Antoinette LaPenna Maas' Easter Pie recipe in the A.C.I.M. cookbook contained macaroni.

In 2002, Giorgilli was interviewed by the Baltimore Sun as she observed a Good Friday procession led by a pastor of St. Leo Roman Catholic Church. The church is a central institution in many of the Little Italy recollections. "Oh, it's beautiful," she sighed, watching from her porch as her granddaughter passed by with the altar girls.

In many parts of the world, Easter is as important a Christian holiday as Christmas, and those customs have been carried on by many of Maryland's immigrant communities. Thankfully, some stories of these holiday traditions have been documented for posterity. The history is also hiding within the various Easter breads, cookies, and pies that families brought with them to Maryland. —KMH

An Easter procession

Torta Pasqualina (Italian Easter pie)

Baltimore City

 main dish

CIAO DOWN

Yields 6 servings

Originally from Liguria, I can really see why this pie would be a hit at Easter anywhere. It is very simple if you, as I did, use prepared puff pastry instead of making your own but very dramatic to slice it open and reveal a perfectly cooked egg on a bed of spinach filling. —RR

INGREDIENTS:

- **32** oz. fresh baby spinach, lightly chopped
- **1** onion, chopped
- **3** cloves garlic, minced
- **15** oz. ricotta cheese
- **5** oz. grated Parmesan cheese
- salt
- freshly ground black pepper
- **¼** teaspoon nutmeg
- **7** eggs (6 for filling and one for brushing the dough)
- **2** sheets frozen puff pastry (1 17.3-oz. box), thawed according to package instructions

ITALIAN EASTER PIE CASSEROLE   Antoinette LaPenna Moss

1 lb. macaroni
2 sticks pepperoni
1 lb. capocollo (sliced and cut into pieces)
1 lb. salami (sliced and cut into pieces)
3 doz. eggs
3 lbs. Ricotta cheese
1/2 c. grated Parmesan cheese
1 lb. white cheese, shredded
1 tsp. black pepper
1 lb. yellow cheese, shredded

Boil macaroni 15 minutes and drain. Combine all ingredients. Bake in shallow pan for approximately 1 1/2 to 2 hours at 325 degrees. Cut into cubes or slices and serve.

DIRECTIONS:

Preheat oven to **350°**.

Oil an 8-inch springform pan with about 3 inch tall sides. Set aside.

Heat a couple of tablespoons of **olive oil** in a large skillet, then sauté the **onion** and **garlic** until the onion is translucent. Stir in about 1/4 of the **spinach** and sauté until it begins to wilt. Sprinkle with **salt**. Keep adding spinach in batches, stirring occasionally, until all is wilted.

Drain off excess water. I like to press it in batches in a metal sieve.

Place in a large bowl, add the **ricotta**, **parmesan**, and **seasoning**. Mix until all ingredients are evenly distributed.

Unroll one sheet of defrosted **pastry** into the bottom of the pan. Press into the bottom and sides to to fully line the pan. Cut off overhang as needed.

Top with spinach mixture. The mixture should come about to the top of the pan.

Using a spoon, make 5 deep wells equidistant around the edges of the pan and one in the middle. Crack an **egg** into each well.

Top with remaining pastry sheet and press closed, using any overhanging scraps as needed to fill in.

Make a tiny divot with the tip of a knife to indicate the sides of each of the five eggs if you want to be sure five people each get a whole egg.

In small bowl, whisk together the yolk with a couple tablespoons of water. Brush over the pastry.

Vent with tip of a knife.

Bake for 55-60 minutes, or until top is golden brown and it's heated though—slide a knife into the center and see if it feels warm when it comes out.

Allow to cool for 30 minutes in the pan on a wire rack before opening and removing the pie from the springform pan.

Slice along the divots to avoid slicing down the middle of an egg if desired.

Serve warm or at room temperature.

Cool any leftovers on the wire rack then wrap tightly in foil and refrigerate for up to two days.

Ambrosia & Nectar
KOULOURAKIA (Easter Cookies)

At the historic Greek Orthodox Cathedral of the Annunciation, parishioners gathered at 11 p.m. on Saturday, May 2nd, 1964. Weeks earlier, Baltimore's other Christian denominations had celebrated Easter. For the city's two Greek Orthodox churches, on a different holy calendar, the 40-day Lenten fast was just coming to an end.

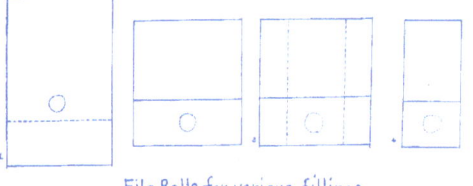

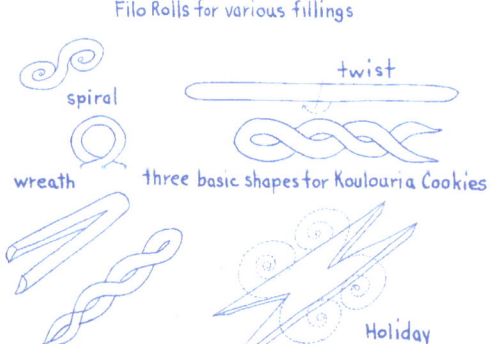

The Evening Sun ran an article in advance of the event, calling it "one of the most exciting religious experiences in Christianity." The story ran alongside a photograph of Rev. Father George Gallos holding a lit candle and looking skyward.

As midnight approached, the lights in the church were turned off, leaving the crowd in hushed anticipation. Soon, the altar doors opened and Gallos emerged with a flame. "Come Partake of the Light," he intoned.

"Christ Has Risen, Trampling Down Death," the hymn began. For the next 40 days, Gallos told the Sun, Christ would be "with the faithful until his ascension."

Following the dramatic midnight service, Baltimore's Greek Orthodox families would gather in their homes, cracking red Easter eggs and feasting on lamb and pastries.

The crispy cookies known as Koulourakia are just one of the many Easter recipes found in cookbooks from the Cathedral and from St. Demetrios Church, located in Parkville. Others include Easter soup with lamb lung, traditional bread studded with red eggs, and Easter Halva, but Koulourakia appear in the greatest numbers and with many variations. A recipe from Georgia Kerasiotes of St. Demitrios in their 1981 "Kali Orexi" (meaning "good appetite") cookbook included ouzo. Anastasia Maggelakis added frozen orange juice concentrate. Georgia Trintis used cream cheese.

Greek Independence Day, St. Nicholas Greek Orthodox Church

Cathedral of the Annunciation's "Ambrosia and Nectar" was published in 1962 as a collective effort, with contributors' names appearing at the front of the book rather than next to the recipes, but that didn't stop them from including 10 different takes on Koulourakia. Some of them called for the cook to obtain the traditional leavening, ammonia.

The cookbook was so successful that the church produced an update called "The Best of Greek Cookery" a decade later. By then, the ammonia had given way to baking powder.

The quantity of Easter recipes in these cookbooks demonstrates the importance of the holiday in the Greek Orthodox church. The many variations are a testament to the myriad ways that cooks put their loving stamp on the most special of occasions. —KMH

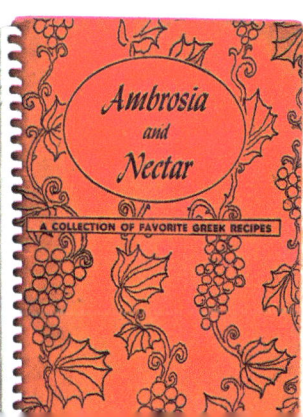

Koulourakia
(Πασχαλινά κουλουράκια)
Greek Easter Cookies

Baltimore City	Yields 3 dozen
sweet dish	

Traditionally made on Holy Thursday to be eaten after Holy Saturday right before Easter, koulourakia are a buttery, crisp cookie that are rolled into short ropes and then braided (the three ropes are said to represent the Holy Trinity) or formed into coils and other shapes. The most common seem to be flavored with orange and vanilla but some people like to flavor them with brandy, ouzo or mastic (a woodsy tasting resin), or make them more savory by topping them with sesame seeds.

Just as there are many flavors and shapes of koulourakia, there are a lot of different techniques of making the dough. To make the cookies extra flakey, I worked cold butter into the flour rather than creaming softened butter and sugar together. I also found this method yielded a dough that was very easy to handle.

I also used a traditional ingredient that is popular in Greece to get the desired super crisp outer layer—bakers' ammonia (ammonium carbonate, also known as hartshorn salt). It is easy to use but has some distinctive traits. It fizzes up when you introduce it to heat and it does smell like ammonia. In this case, we add it to warm milk and it quickly degrades to gaseous ammonia and carbon dioxide which causes it to fizz and then when added to the dough, leavens the cookies. It is only used when making small crisp baked goods like crackers or cookies because it needs to "escape" into the air, not get trapped in heavy batters. The smell dissipates quickly and there is no trace of any ammonia flavor in the finished cookies. —RR

While you can substitute baking powder for the baker's ammonia in a 1:1 ratio, it is easier to find than you may think and worth checking out. It is used in a variety of cookies like German pfeffernüsse or springerle, Icelandic loftkökur, Danish brunkager and Norwiegian sirupsnipper, among others, as well as in some crackers. Mediterranean, European and baking specialty stores sell it as well as many online retailers and the craft store chain Michael's.

HOLIDAY TRADITIONS FROM THE OLD LINE STATE

INGREDIENTS:

- **8** tablespoons cold butter, cut into small cubes
- **4 ⅓** cups flour
- **½** teaspoon of baking soda
- **1** cup sugar
- **¼** teaspoon of salt
- **½** cup milk
- **¾** teaspoon bakers' ammonia
- **2** eggs
- **1** teaspoon vanilla
- zest from 1 orange
- **¼** cup fresh orange juice (about 1 orange worth of juice)

EGG WASH

- **1** egg
- **1** tablespoon water

DIRECTIONS:

In the bowl of a stand-mixer whisk together **flour**, **baking soda**, **sugar**, and **salt**.

Add the **cold butter** and mix until the flour looks textured with tiny clumps.

In a small saucepan warm the **milk** slightly. Remove from heat and stir in the baker's **ammonia**. It will foam up! It smells like ammonia! Do not be alarmed.

Add the milk mixture, **eggs**, **vanilla**, **zest**, and **juice** to the flour mixture and mix until a thick dough forms.

If it is warm out, refrigerate the dough about 20 minutes until it is easily handled.

Take a small ball of dough, about an inch and an half wide and use your hands to roll it into a snake about ¼ inch thick. Coil, braid or make shapes with your snake.

Place the shapes on the lined cookie sheets.

Whisk the egg wash ingredients together and brush on the cookies.

Bake at **375°** about 12-15 minutes or until golden brown.

Cool completely in the pans on wire racks, flipping the cookies after 10 minutes.

Store in airtight containers.

Esther Baral's
BLINTZES

When Esther Baral was a young girl in East Baltimore, her neighbors hailed from Russia, Poland, and Romania. Their lingua franca was Yiddish.

As families like Esther's made their way to the local Synagogues, Henry Einspruch, a Polish Jew who had converted to Lutheranism, could often be found outside, preaching the gospel in Yiddish with the assistance of his wife Marie, whose native language of Pennsylvania Dutch enabled her to understand the similar Germanic dialect. An East Baltimore scene if ever there was one.

Einspruch may have gained converts to his nearby church, but Esther's family was not among them. Her father, Nathan Rosenblum, immigrated from Russia in 1904 and found work in Baltimore as a tailor. Two years later, he sent for his wife Lena and three young children. The family settled at 1814 Fayette Street. Four more children were born in the following years. Esther was the youngest girl, born in 1912.

By 1930 the family had relocated to Park Heights in Northwest Baltimore. In this burgeoning middle-class Jewish community, people from Austria and Russia settled alongside American-born Jews. Here, the primary language spoken was English, peppered with Yiddish, Hebrew, German, and Eastern European languages.

Esther went on to earn an M.S.W. from the University of Pennsylvania and then became a social worker back in Baltimore. She married Philadelphian Leon Baral, also the son of Russian immigrants. In a 1960s Baltimore Sun interview, she told reporter Helen Henry about her work helping impoverished people navigate the hundreds of resources in the city. "To understand welfare one must also understand economics and political science," she said.

Blintzes, Esther told Henry, were an anytime dish, "easy to prepare." They were, if the title of the column is to be taken literally, her "Favorite Recipe."

Esther's mother taught her to make the rolled pancakes with cheese filling. She later learned that her recipe "is the same one used by Romanian and Polish cooks, as well as Russian." Perhaps this had included her East Baltimore or Park Heights neighbors. There were many variations, Esther said. "They are all good."

There are different stories about why dairy dishes like blintzes are eaten on Shavuot. Some say it symbolizes the "land flowing with milk and honey." Others say that after the Torah was given on Mt. Sinai - the event Shavuot commemorates - the people did not want to eat their meat since it had not been prepared in accordance with their newly-understood dietary laws.

Whether or not Esther made her beloved blintzes for the "Feast of Weeks," many other people eat the dish on that day; its cheese filling satisfies the custom of eating dairy. Tradition is a good excuse to enjoy your favorite recipe. —KMH

Mrs. Leon Baral preparing a plate of blintzes

Suburban House Restaurant
next to Pikes Theatre, Pikesville
Crab Meat Blintzes
Crab Meat Blintzes
Crab Meat Blintzes
—only at Gordon's
of Orleans Street
Even wild horses

 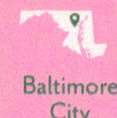

Baltimore City

FEAST OF WEEKS

 sweet dish | Yields 9 blintzes

Cheese Blintz with Blueberry Sauce

Blintzes are surprisingly simple to make. While they are traditionally made with farmers or pot cheese (sort of a dry cottage cheese), I find drained ricotta yields excellent, near identical results and is easier to source. I like to use the same 10-inch crêpe pan I use to make buckwheat crêpes for slightly oversized blintzes, but you can use a 6-inch pan to make a classic two-bite blintz. —**RR**

If you use a 6-inch pan instead, make the recipe as-is but halve the amount of batter and filling used for each individual blintz to yield about 18.

INGREDIENTS:

FOR THE SAUCE:
- 1 quart blueberries (fresh or frozen)
- ¼ cup sugar
- ¼ cup water

FOR THE FILLING:
- 16 oz whole milk ricotta (drained overnight through a sieve over a bowl in the refrigerator, discard liquid)
- 8 oz cream cheese, at room temperature
- 1 egg, at room temperature
- 2 tablespoons sugar
- 1 teaspoon vanilla

FOR THE BATTER:
- 3 eggs, at room temperature
- 1 cup milk, at room temperature
- ¾ cup flour, sifted
- 1 tablespoon sugar
- 2 tablespoons canola oil (or butter, melted and cooled)
- Pinch salt

DIRECTIONS:

In a small saucepan, heat the **sauce ingredients** until the blueberries break down and form a loose, rustic sauce, about 5 minutes. Add more water if needed to yield a spoonable sauce. Keep on low to keep warm as you make the blintz.

Meanwhile, in a medium bowl, whisk together all the **filling ingredients** until very smooth. **Set aside**.

In medium bowl, whisk together the **batter ingredients** until very smooth.

Heat some **butter** in a 10-inch crêpe pan. Add about ¼ cup of batter just to coat the bottom of the pan. Swirl in a circular motion to coat. Cook for about 1-2 minutes or until browned on the bottom. Remove to a platter and place in a single layer (or in multiple layers separated by parchment) while you make the remaining of the batter.

Fill the blini (pancakes) by placing about ½ cup filling in the center, browned side up. Close by folding the bottom and top side up over the filling and then the sides to make a rectangular packet. Repeat for remaining blini. The pale side of the blini should be on the outside of the filled blintz.

On a griddle or large skillet, heat some butter and pan fry each blintz on each side until the centers are cooked through and they are golden brown.

Serve immediately with blueberry sauce spooned on top.

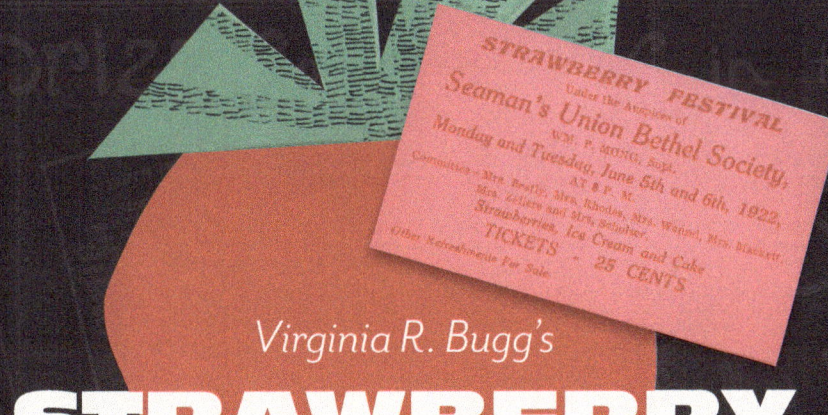

Virginia R. Bugg's
STRAWBERRY COBBLER

"Once upon a time, people were wont to talk about the strawberry season and to look forward to it with delightful expectation. It brought visions of strawberry shortcake with mashed berries... and there was the social angle, the strawberry festival which brought together the elite of the neighborhood... Gone are these amenities, sacrificed beneath the juggernaut wheels of advancing science... In Europe, where national boundaries are close together and national self-sufficiency is a coddled ideal, seasons for strawberries are well-defined and short..."

Throughout the warmer months, Marylanders assemble excitedly around tables to welcome the waves of fresh fruits and vegetables arriving from our fields. The strawberry, as one of the first fruits of spring, has been the subject of celebrations since long before the colonization of the Americas. Among many Native peoples, strawberries were considered a gift or blessing from the Creator.

Strawberry dances and festivals were held as the fruits began to ripen each year.

Later, savvy church women's groups in the mid-1800s used strawberry festivals as another tool in the arsenal of fundraising strategies along with cookbooks, suppers, raffles, and staged performances.

Newspapers ran paid ads, but also dropped mentions of strawberry festivals within their pages.

A festival held in June of 1852 promised to be "in every respect, delightful." "Do go," the Baltimore Sun commanded. In 1861 they more crassly suggested that strawberry festivals were full of "delicious fruit and pretty women!"

The Cecil Whig promised that an 1863 festival would feature "ice cream, strawberries, and the usual delicacies of the season… at moderate prices."

An 1870 article in the Easton Star-Democrat offered a glimpse of what went on at these festivals. With the aim of "[pleasing] those who were present by reminding them of the pleasures of the occasion, and to make those who were not regret their absence," the writer went into excruciating detail on the size and arrangement of the rooms. They described "elegant cakes" which "lifted their snowy apexes above the gorgeous scarlet of the berries," and "flowers of every hue and variety." Tables were decked with flowers in imitation of garden landscaping and the "beauty of the flowers was surpassed by the beauty of the smiling faces" of the hosts.

Cakes were auctioned off. Despite the rain, attendees came from Baltimore by steamboat. Music was provided by a string band assisted by an organ.

The Afro-American ran reports on strawberry festivals held by Black organizations, both locally and around the country. In 1909 they announced that a strawberry festival held by the "Fresh Air Circle" raised about $2500 (adjusted for inflation). The Fresh Air Circle was a group of women who operated a farm for impoverished children to visit in the summer (essentially a summer camp) near Reisterstown.

Strawberry sorters packing crates, 1920s

Strawberry festivals weren't exclusive to Maryland, but Maryland had special reason to celebrate the annual crop. Indigenous species of strawberries didn't thrive here, but later cultivars derived from the strawberries of several continents became a fruit well-suited to local farms. "Strawberry Fever" took hold in the U.S., and Anne Arundel County was at one time "the most important strawberry district in the South," according to Willard R. Mumford in "Strawberries, Peas, & Beans: Truck farming in Anne Arundel County." There was fierce competition, much of it from within the state. On the Eastern Shore, Marion Station in Somerset County was said to be the "Strawberry Capital of the World."

> **"In this country, good ripe strawberries at a reasonable price are to be had in the depths of winter, long before strawberry plants have blossomed in Anne Arundel gardens... Good old strawberry, long may she wave!"**
> – Evening Capital, 1940 (Annapolis)

Strawberries were singled out by the Baltimore Sun in 1911 when the paper held a series of weekly recipe contests. Each week had a theme: soups, pickles, cakes, etc. For a few weeks, the themes were specific ingredients: potatoes, tomatoes, crabs, and strawberries. The recipe adapted here comes via Virginia R. Bugg (1883-1967) of 1801 Regester Street, who won an honorable mention for her strawberry cobbler, with sweetened strawberries drizzled in orange juice, topped with "rich paste."

Although Maryland hosted the highest acreage of strawberries in the nation in 1910, "Strawberry Fever" soon caused overproduction, which led to a price decline. As the food system—and strawberries themselves— changed, strawberries from elsewhere could travel longer distances and reach tables earlier than those grown in Maryland. This, combined with a few years of unfortunate weather, caused the local strawberry industry to take a dive.

Maryland strawberry production may have fizzled out, but the tradition of strawberry festivals remains. Each spring, dozens of towns, churches and farms hold gatherings to celebrate the ripening fruit that marks the approach of summer, and all the good food that comes with it. —KMH

Strawberry Cobbler

Maryland

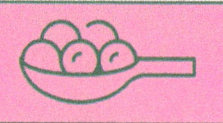
Yields 6-8 servings

sweet dish

There are all sorts of cobblers—biscuity ones, cakey ones, dumpling topped ones—this one has a sheet of crispy pastry on top and is possibly the fastest, easiest cobbler ever.
—**RR**

INGREDIENTS:

- **8** cups sliced fresh or defrosted, frozen strawberries
- zest from 1 orange
- **3** tablespoons instant tapioca
- **3** tablespoons orange juice
- **⅔** cup sugar
- **1** sheet frozen puff pastry, thawed according to package instructions

DIRECTIONS:

Preheat oven to **400°**. Lightly butter a shallow 3-quart baking dish. Set aside.

In a large bowl bowl, toss together the **strawberries, zest, tapioca, orange juice** and **sugar**. Allow to sit 10 minutes. Toss again. Pour the mixture into the dish.

Top with the pastry. Use the end of a knife to make slits into the top to allow for steam to escape.

Bake for 20 minutes or until golden brown and bubbly.

Cool on wire rack for 10 minutes prior to serving.

Community cookbooks used to include blank pages for the book's owners to jot down extra recipes. The cookbook creators expected each copy to take on a life of its own in someone's kitchen; to be spattered on and scribbled in. The printed recipes were just a starting point.

Since conducting the research for this book, I've been asking people about the special foods they make and eat for holidays, birthdays, summer cookouts, and other special occasions. I've heard about recipes that have been handed down for generations, and watched as people got wistful looks while remembering long-ago meals. I've felt so lucky to have these conversations.

Others have told me, almost apologetically, about a dish they've been making for only a few years, remarking that their chosen fare is not particularly special or interesting. On the contrary, those are some of my favorites!

Your gathering could be an excuse to cook something impractical, to lure a special guest to the table, or to celebrate a garden harvest. Your festive recipe could be in the early stages of being perfected, made with ingredients that would baffle your great-grandmother, and shared with a family you built on your own. Some traditions are worn-in and seasoned by time, but others are just being born. —**KMH**

Let the spattering and scribbling commence.

WHAT'S COOKIN' _____ **SERVES** _____

FROM THE KITCHEN OF _____

BIBLIOGRAPHY

American Committee on Italian Migration. Italian American Favorite Recipes. 1982.

Annunciation Greek Orthodox Community. Ambrosia and Nectar. 1962.

Bethel A.M.E. Church. Bethel Cookbook. Baltimore, MD. 1979.

Citizens for Progress St. Mary's County. 300 Years of Black Cooking in St. Mary's County Maryland. 1975.

Dorot Jewish Division, The New York Public Library. Pots, pans and pie-plates and how to use them. The New York Public Library Digital Collections. 1905.

Elizabeth Ellicott Lea. Domestic cookery, useful receipts, and hints to young housekeepers. 2004.

Frederick Philip Stieff. Eat, Drink & Be Merry In Maryland. Johns Hopkins University Press. Baltimore, MD. 1998.

Gaskins, Ruth L.. A Good Heart and a Light Hand. United States, Fund for Alexandria, Virginia, 1968.

Glasse, Hannah. The Art of Cookery Made Plain and Easy. United Kingdom, W. Strahan [and 25 others], 1784.

Hagerstown Branch Relief Society Organization, Church of Jesus Christ of Latter-Day Saints. Favorite Recipes. 1975.

Hammond-Harwood House Association. Maryland's Way. The Hammond-Harwood House Association. 1966.

Hampstead Ward (Church of Jesus Christ of Latter-Day Saints). Priceless Treasures. 1980s.

Harvey, Katherine A. "The Lonaconing Journals: The Founding of a Coal and Iron Community, 1837-1840." Transactions of the American Philosophical Society, vol. 67, no. 2, 1977

Helen Henry. My Favorite Recipe. 1968.

John Gilman D'Arcy Paul manuscript collection, MS 3108. H. Furlong Baldwin Library.

John Shields. Chesapeake Bay Cooking with John Shields. Broadway Books. New York, NY. 1998.

Korfhage, Matthew. "Born during Slavery, Spicy Stuffed Ham Now Graces Every Southern Maryland Table." Yahoo, Yahoo, 13 Apr. 2022.

Lewis, Edna. The Taste of Country Cooking: The 30th Anniversary Edition of a Great Southern Classic Cookbook. Knopf Doubleday Publishing Group, 2006.

Little Italy Lodge. Let's Cook Italian. 1990s.

Little Italy, 4. Baltimore Neighborhood Heritage Project, R0014-BNHP. Baltimore Regional Studies Archives.

Livie, Kate. Chesapeake Oysters: The Bay's Foundation and Future. Arcadia Publishing, 2015.

Maryland Home Economics Association. Maryland Cooking. 1948.

MCHS Staff/Curator. Exhibit Research: "Small Town Jewish Life in Montgomery County". Montgomery County Historical Society. 2003-2004.

Miller, Adrian. Soul Food. UNC Press Books, 2013.

Mitzvah Chapter B'Nai B'Rith Women of Columbia. Pick of the Crop. 1976.

Mothers Club of St. Wenceslaus Catholic Church. Recipes from "Little Bohemia". 1984.

Mrs. Benjamin Chew Howard. Fifty Years in a Maryland Kitchen. J. B. Lippincott Co. 1873.

Mrs. Charles H. Gibson. Mrs. Charles H. Gibson's Maryland And Virginia Cookbook. John Murphy & Co.. Baltimore. 1894.

Mrs. J. H. Giese. The Practical Cook Book. Hanzche & Company. Batimore. 1888.

Mumford, Willard R. "Strawberries, Peas, & Beans: Truck farming in Anne Arundel County." 2000.

Prescott, Marianne Holman. "Erastus Snow: Faithful Servant, Missionary and Colonizer." Church News, Church News, 23 Feb. 2013,

Priebe, Gregory, et al. Forgotten Maryland Cocktails: A History of Drinking in the Free State. History Press, 2015.

Rappaport, Rachel. Coconut & Lime, https://www.coconutandlime.com/.

Reber, Patricia Bixler. Researching Food History, http://researchingfoodhistory.blogspot.com/.

Sherman, Elisabeth. "How Sauerkraut Became Baltimore's Traditional Thanksgiving Side." Matador Network. 4 Nov. 2020.

Shields, David. "The return of PIE WARS —SWEET POTATO V. PUMPKIN." Facebook, 12 Oct. 2017.

SlackWater, Series 8.8. SMCM Publications records, RG 08. St. Mary's College of Maryland Archives.

Southern Heritage Cookbook Library. All Pork (Southern Heritage). Oxmoor House. Birmingham, AL. 1984.

Southern Heritage Cookbook Library. Family Gatherings (Southern Heritage). Oxmoor House. Birmingham, AL. 1984.

Southern Heritage Cookbook Library. Pies & Pastry (Southern Heritage). Oxmoor House. Birmingham, AL. 1984.

St. Demetrious Greek Orthodox Church of Baltimore. Kali Orexi. 1990.

Symington-Slingluff Papers, 1866-1980. MS 2934. H. Furlong Baldwin Library.

Tipton-Martin, Toni. The Jemima Code. University of Texas Press, 2015.

Tkacik, Christina. "A Taste of Home for Baltimore's Lumbee Tribe Members." Baltimore Sun, 31 May 2019.

Twitty, Michael W. Fighting Old Nep: Foodways of Enslaved Afro-Marylanders, 1634-1864. United States, n.p, 2006.

Twitty, Michael W. The Cooking Gene: A Journey Through African American Culinary History in the Old South. HarperCollins, 2018.

Twitty, Michael W Koshersoul: The Faith and Food Journey of an African American Jew. AMISTAD, 2022.

UNC Pembroke. "Honoring Native Foodways." The University of North Carolina at Pembroke, 19 Aug. 2022.

White, Joyce. A Taste of History, https://atasteofhistory.net/.

Women's Welsh Club of Baltimore. Favorite Recipes from the Women's Welsh Club of Baltimore. 1980.

Women's Club Of Melwood District. The Melwood Cook Book. Rosaryville, MD. 1920.

Women's Fellowship of Bethel Korean Church. Ladies of the Bethel. Morris Press. 1986.

Annapolis Capital Gazette; The Baltimore Afro-American; Baltimore Sun/ Evening Sun; Baltimore City Paper; Chicago Weekly Post; The Cumberland News; The Food Timeline; The Frederick News Post; Internet Archive; Los Angeles Times; The New York Times; The Staunton Spectator; Wikipedia.

Images sourced for this book were supplied by the following institutions, organizations and people:

Baltimore Museum of Industry, Baltimore Sun, Bertha Hunt, Chesapeake Maritime Museum, Creative Commons, East Baltimore Documentary Photography Project, Enoch Pratt Free Library, I. Henry Phillips Sr., Jewish Museum of Maryland, Library of Congress, Maryland Center for History and Culture, Maryland State Archives, Edward H. Nabb Research Center for Delmarva History and Culture at Salisbury University, Paul C. Liebe, Paul Henderson Photograph Collection. Baltimore City Life Museum Collection of the Maryland Historical Society, University of Maryland Baltimore County, University of Maryland Special Collections, Wellcome Collection

www.ingramcontent.com/pod-product-compliance
Lightning Source LLC
Chambersburg PA
CBHW061357010526
44107CB00012B/961